# Discovering the Joy

## Of representing Jesus in everyday life

ANDREW CHALMERS



ISBN: 9798579809773

# DEDICATION

I dedicate this book to my dad and mom, Louis and Nancy Chalmers. Even when everything seemed hopeless, they endured with me through some of the hardest moments in my life and continued to pray for me. I am eternally grateful for them and the example they have been in my life of God's grace and love. I honor you and love you both!

# CONTENTS

# ENDORSEMENTS

"*Discover the Joy*" is an open door, beckoning you to step into more of the abundant life for which you were created. Filled with inspiring stories, biblical insights, and proven principles, these pages point you to living a more Jesus-shaped life which produces good fruit that lasts. Andrew Chalmers is a living example of the joyful and impactful way of life this book describes, and through his testimony he offers you practical steps that will help you follow Jesus more closely."

**– Bob Rognlien**

Author of *Recovering the Way* and *A Jesus-Shaped Life*

"Andrew Chalmers shares the kind of evangelism we have practiced and valued for four decades on the mission field — one that flows from personal intimacy with Jesus, from a prayerful life in God's presence. It is an invitation to a fresh identity in the family of God, the life we value above everything in this world. If you want to be a worker in this harvest, be blessed by his wisdom and testimony."

**– Heidi G. Baker, Ph.D.**

Co-founder and Executive Chairman of the Board, Iris Global

"The joy of knowing Jesus and the privilege that we have to share the good news with others at times is breathtaking. "*Discovering the Joy*" by Andrew Chalmers will point you to the source of all true Joy and that is Jesus. There are very few equipping evangelists like Andrew Chalmers that not only desire to see the lost saved but also desire for the church to enter into the joy of knowing Jesus and making Him known to this generation. When we only have one life to live, we live in such a way that makes sense in the light of eternity. I can get behind this book because it reflects the heart of God for us and for those that don't know Him yet. My encouragement to you is that this book will become a tool for you to learn from, put into practice what you have learnt so that you can teach others as well. May God bless you."

**– Chris Overstreet**

Founder, Compassion to Action

# ACKNOWLEDGMENTS

I want to say a special thank you to my wife, Ellen Chalmers, who was willing to watch the kids while I went away several times to work on this manuscript. Her encouragement has been so needed throughout the process of working on this project. I want to thank Karissa Corpeny for being a coach and an enormous encouragement along the way. Her input and feedback have helped me bring my thoughts and teachings together in a book format. I am so grateful for the editing and feedback that Sherri Foarde has provided. It is a much better book because of her. My entire team at Take the City and so many friends and family have been incredibly supportive of me during this long process. Thank you all for believing in me and encouraging me to finish. I want to thank my pastor, Paul Thomas, who took the time to read the entire manuscript and then reviewed it with me to ensure the book was theologically sound and that the content flowed well together. His help meant more to me than I can express with words. Lastly, I want to thank Holy Spirit for inviting me on this incredible journey of discovering the joy of representing Jesus in my everyday life.

# INTRODUCTION

## We Long for Adventure and Greater Joy

One of life's greatest ambitions is the pursuit of true and lasting joy—the kind of joy that transcends our circumstances. For years, I searched for joy, only to end up going down many dead-end roads. I thought I would discover joy in finding the right relationships, experiences or accomplishments. What I found instead was new levels of disappointment in things I thought would surely satisfy my longing for joy.

For years, I was bound by an addiction to drugs and other things because I was searching for a deep and lasting joy. Eventually, I wound up losing everything. In 2009, I found myself homeless, addicted to heroin and on the brink of suicide. In November of that year, I reached a major turning point. This book tells the story of how God invited me on an incredible journey.

So many of us remain distracted by fleeting pleasures, accomplishments and things that never truly satisfy. We were created with a deeper longing—a longing for pure joy that is sustained no matter what we face in our lives. This desire for joy was placed inside our hearts by God and can only be satisfied when we discover that it comes from being in relationship and partnering with Him in His purposes on the earth.

I invite you into a rhythm and way of living that will change how you live life. I hope that my experiences will either spur you on in your own journey or will instill a desire in you to discover, maybe for the first time, the joy of representing Jesus in your everyday life.

To begin our journey together, I want to share a story that will provide a glimpse into where we are headed…

## Fortune Tellers at a Festival

Several years ago, I was leading a training on evangelism in Harrisburg, Pennsylvania. After a few hours of teaching and activities, we went into the streets where a large festival was being held in the downtown area next to the riverfront. We split up into teams and went all over the area, starting up conversations and praying for people as we shared the gospel.

After a meaningful conversation with one of the festival vendors, I stepped back to watch the other teams ministering to people all over. It was amazing to see so many people open to prayer and hearing the gospel at the same time. While I was standing off to the side, I felt Holy Spirit begin to nudge me to look up the hill to a particular vendor. I sensed the Lord prompting me to go to their tent to offer prayer and minister.

As I got closer to the tent, I saw that this particular vendor was quite different from the others. It was a fortune-telling tent with two women sitting behind a table, reading palms and tarot cards for people attending the festival. When I realized what they were doing, I honestly wanted to turn around and go the other way. What was I going to say to some tarot card readers? With no idea how to strike up a conversation, I was obedient and walked over until I stood in front of their table. The younger of the two women smiled and asked me, "Would you like to have your palm read?"

I wasn't interested in having my palm read and I still didn't know what to say. As I stood there for a few moments, she asked me again. Now it was getting awkward. I began to silently pray for God to come and show me what to say.

Just before she asked me a third time, I sensed Holy Spirit leading me to ask the older woman sitting behind the table a question. "Ma'am, do you have an issue in the center of your lower back that is hurting you?"

Looking up at me with a puzzled look, she said, "Yes, why?"

Suddenly a rush of faith filled my heart. Now I felt a boldness as I stood at the tarot card reading table. I responded, "God led me to your table and showed me that you had an issue with your back. I was wondering if I could pray for you."

She agreed to let me come over to her and pray. Afterward, she said she immediately felt all the pain leave her back as she stood from her chair. I was shocked, she was shocked and so was the young woman. Looking at her now, I sensed God wanted me to share some words with her. As He led, I spoke. I could hear the older woman gasping as God obviously showed me things that were otherwise impossible for me to know. The more I stepped out in faith, the more Holy Spirit used me.

Then suddenly, I felt released and an urge to leave. I finished the conversation, prayed for both of them and walked away. It felt like I had just been living in some sort of dream. I had no idea what God was going to do and as I walked down the hill, I took a deep breath and sat down next to a tree, thanking God for all He was doing through the teams sharing the gospel at the festival. It was then that my friend Dennis came up to me.

"I've been looking for you!," he said. "There's a lady at a tent where they do palm readings who has been asking for you. She wants to talk to you right now."

A little puzzled as to why one of the women from the tent would want to talk to me again, I wondered if they were angry with me or that I had said something wrong. I followed Dennis back to the tarot card tent.

When we arrived, there was a different woman under the tent by herself. She invited us into the tent and came toward me to give me a big motherly hug. I was confused, but hugged back and greeted her.

She said, "I have heard many good things about you. My family has told me what you said and all the things that happened and I wanted to meet you. I am the mother of this family and I have sent them to gather our entire family to come here to the tent. We want to hear more of what you have to say."

I was in shock.

As we waited for the rest of her family to come, the woman insisted on buying us lunch. When they arrived, she gathered all of them together and asked me to speak. Over the next 15 minutes or so, I shared some of my testimony and the gospel with them. Then I told them that if any of them wanted to be saved, they could surrender their lives to Jesus Christ right then and there. Every person in the family, except one young man, responded to the gospel and were born again right there next to the tarot card tent!

Afterward, we all rejoiced and I began to disciple them further in their faith. I gave them my number and asked them to call me later so we could connect more. I felt so joyful. As I left this encounter, I was blown away that God had allowed me to be a part of such a life-changing experience for an entire family.

A few months later, I was in our office with some of our team when my phone rang. The person on the phone shared with me that she was the woman who I had met under the tarot card tent a few months before in Pennsylvania.

She explained that she had a niece who had come to their house and was in need of help. She told her niece that if she would talk to me, she could also hear the same message they had heard months before that had so deeply touched them. After her niece got on the phone, I was put on speaker phone for the rest of their extended family to hear. During the call, I got a chance to share the gospel again and the niece responded in faith after hearing the good news!

The joy I experienced during this divine connection was indescribable. Being able to see this entire family encounter the love of God, hear the good news of Jesus Christ and then respond was beyond satisfying. It was as if I was created to live this way and to represent Jesus in my everyday life.

# 1 - DISCOVERING THE JOY

The purpose of this book is to share my journey of discovering the joy of representing Jesus and the experiences that come with it. God not only desires for me to live in a right relationship with Him but to be a vessel that He can use to invite others to know Him as well. This entire book is an invitation to come along and discover this joy for yourself.

In John 4 we find a story that has been foundational in the journey and in the writing of this book. Jesus takes His disciples along with Him on a journey and they ended up stopping in a city called Sychar. When they arrive, the disciples go into the city to get some food and Jesus stays alone outside of the city near a watering well. A woman comes out of the city in the middle of the day to retrieve water and He begins to talk to her. He asks her to get him some water and then tells her that if she actually knew who He was, she would be asking Him for "living water."

After spending time with Jesus, she realizes that she wants this living water and that He is much more than just an ordinary man. Eventually, she understands that He is the promised Messiah they have been waiting for and goes to get the others to come and meet Him. This woman, who had a tainted past, becomes one of the first persons in the Bible who brings others to Jesus.

Toward the end of the story, we see the disciples returning from finding food and they ask the Lord if He is ready to eat. Jesus responds to them that, after this divine appointment with the woman, He has already had some food that they don't know anything about. I can only imagine the confusion they experienced when He said that He had already had some food. They had just spent most of the day going into the city to get some food because, obviously, they had run out earlier that day. After seeing their confusion and sparking their curiosity, Jesus reveals to them a key that will lay a foundation for this entire book.

Jesus tells them plainly, "My food is to do the will of him who sent me and to accomplish his work. Do you not say, 'There are yet four months, then comes the harvest'? Look, I tell you, lift up your eyes, and see that the fields are white for harvest. Already the one who reaps is receiving wages and gathering fruit for eternal life, so that sower and reaper may rejoice together. For here the saying holds true, 'One sows and another reaps.' I sent you to reap that for which you did not labor. Others have labored, and you have entered into their labor" (John 4:34-38).

Jesus reveals that He finds true satisfaction and fulfillment from doing the will of His father. He uses the illustration of laboring for a harvest as being the food that fills Him. He uses this illustration to point the disciples to the greater reality for which we are all created.

## Water and Food

What we discover from this simple story is that there are two key elements to sustain life that Jesus uses to teach this woman and His disciples.

### WATER

The first element to sustain life that He brings up is water. He does this to teach us that when we come to Him, we can gain eternal, life-giving water that will never run dry. This life-giving water that springs up to eternal life is for all those who come to Him. This life-giving water illustrates the spiritual reality that we can only gain eternal life and joy when we connect to God through His son Jesus Christ.

The water points us to our internal need for connection and intimacy with our creator God. We were created to know God. Our sin, however, has separated us all from that which we were made for. We cannot know God because of this separation. Jesus came to break down this barrier and wall of separation by laying down his own life and taking the punishment we deserved for our sin. This is the good news we discover in the Bible! We can now be restored back into what we were originally created because of Jesus Christ.

While we are living lives tainted by sin and shame, we are separated from the water we were created to drink from. When we receive forgiveness of our sins and put our faith in Jesus, we can come to God and freely drink from the water of eternal life. Every human being that has ever lived was created by God with a desperate need for this spiritual water and will not be satisfied with joy and peace until they drink of it. Jesus came to make a way for us to partake of the living water we were made to be fueled and sustained by!

### FOOD

The second element to sustain life that Jesus uses in this story is food. He uses something that we can all relate to and understand to point to a greater spiritual need. We can all relate to having a need for food. We have all experienced hunger from one degree to another.

Jesus uses the example of food to point to a greater need inside each person. God has placed a need and a desire to walk in obedience and to do His will on the earth. Jesus told his disciples that the food that satisfied him the most was doing the will of the Father and reaping a harvest of souls.

There is a measure of joy, satisfaction, and fulfillment that humanity can only discover when we all begin to taste the food of doing the will of the father. We have been created with an innate need to participate in God's redemptive plan on earth. Until we taste this food, we will never be satisfied.

## Communion and Purpose

Jesus came not only to give access to a relationship with God and eternal life, but also to restore us to our God-given purpose that was established from the Garden of Eden. Adam and Eve were able to enjoy a perfect relationship with God before they fell into sin and rebellion. They were also able to experience great joy as they partnered with God to fulfill His plan on the earth. From the very beginning, God established a need in the hearts of all of humanity for two key things: *communion* and *purpose.*

I love the way that Bob Rognlien paints this picture in his book, *Empowering Missional Disciples.*[1] In his book he discusses two key biblical themes that run throughout the entire Bible: Covenant and Kingdom.

The biblical theme of covenant he discusses points to man's innate need for connection with God and how God uses covenant to help establish and restore relationships with mankind. We see that when Jesus ratified the new covenant in His blood on the cross, we were restored into a relationship with God.

He also talks about the biblical theme of kingdom, which points to man's innate need to participate in God's redemptive plans to establish His kingdom in the earth. We were created not to merely exist and be in a relationship with God, but He has also placed a deep desire in each of us to expand His Kingdom and His purposes.

## Sin's perversion of our two primary God-given needs.

After mankind fell into sin, our God-given needs were no longer being met. We were created for intimacy with God but sin was now separating us. That's why so many people fall into a false sense of connection and intimacy through sinful and unhealthy relationships, fornication, adultery, and homosexuality. We're all looking to have this void filled and sin has caused us to pervert these God-given desires and look to other things that cannot truly satisfy.

Thankfully, Jesus has made a way for us to be restored back into communion with God and to drink the *living water* that actually fulfills and sustains us. In Him, we are liberated from the shameful

---

1 Rognlien, Bob. Empowering Missional Disciples: an Introduction to 3D Movements. 3DM Publishing, 2016.

ways that once held us bound and can find true intimacy and connection with God and others.

Just like our need for connection was perverted by sin, so also our need for purpose. God gave us a desire to do great things and to change the world. This is most clearly expressed in the desire within every human being for our lives to matter and carry some form of significance. This desire for significance is not inherently bad. In fact, the desire was placed in us by God Himself when He created mankind in the Garden of Eden. In the Garden he not only placed Adam and Eve there to exist and be in relationship, but to also be fruitful, multiply and subdue the entire earth until the whole planet was like the Garden of Eden.

Sin has perverted this desire for purpose and significance. Many times we strain and strive for success in our own strength and for our own purposes. Many people spend their entire lives seeking adventure and accomplishments, trying to fill this God-given void. Yet even the most successful people remain empty and void of true, lasting joy. No amount of fame, money, or accomplishments will ever truly satisfy. Since our need for purpose came *from* God, it can only be satisfied *by* God.

## Let's go on a journey...

Through this book, I invite you on a journey of discovery. We're going to explore some of the key ways that we access the joy of knowing God and representing Him in our lives. As we explore various topics and passages, I want you to see each chapter as an invitation. My hope is that this book is not merely information or inspiration but that it acts as a catalyst for your life. My prayer is that your life overflows with joy and adventure.

We are not promised that our journey in following Jesus will be easy but we definitely should not expect it to be boring. If we look at the lives of the early disciples, we see lives that were everything but boring. The more we walk in intimacy with Jesus and obey his calling on our lives to go and make disciples, the more we will experience the joy and adventure that our hearts crave.

May we all be "hearers of the Word" AND "doers of the Word" (James 1:22). When we step into our missional calling and destinies to partner with God, we access joy unspeakable.

# 2 - DISCOVERING IDENTITY

> "*...the most portentous fact about any man is not what he at a given time may say or do, but what he in his deep heart conceives God to be like.*" - *A.W. Tozer*[2]

When my son Landon was around 7 years old he decided he wanted to play little league baseball. So, in the spring of that year my wife and I did all that was needed to register and get my son ready for the season. I was excited for him and our family was looking forward to the enjoyment of watching him play. From the time he could walk he had loved baseball. I remember taking him to the ball field as a toddler and he would run around the bases, his young heart thrilled as he imagined himself playing the game. A few years later, around the age of five or six, he had the chance to play T-ball and absolutely loved it. Now he was ready for the "big leagues."

When we took him to tryouts, I remember him being both nervous and excited. I was probably feeling just as nervous and excited as I watched him run around on the field, catch the balls and throw them back to the coaches. I was proud as I watched him, because for years he and I had been playing catch together and I knew he had a strong arm. I was excited for the season to get started after the tryouts, and as any father would, wanted my son to do well.

About a week after tryouts, I took him to practice to watch how he played with the other boys. I was thrilled to see that he was able to catch the ball and throw as well as any of the other boys.

---

2 The Knowledge of the Holy (New York: HarperCollins, 1978), 1.

Unfortunately, my excitement quickly came to a halt when they took the boys to the batting cages to practice hitting.

I hadn't thought about working on hitting the ball. His only experience was playing T-ball where the ball was placed onto a "tee" and the kids just hit the sitting ball. In T-ball, even if you miss the ball and hit the plastic "tee" and the ball falls off, you get to run the bases. As I was watching my son in the batting cage for the first time, I quickly realized this was not T-ball, nor was my son prepared in any way to hit the ball being pitched to him.

I watched as he awkwardly stood next to the plate and tried swinging the bat over and over again at balls slowly coming towards him in the batting cages. The longer practice went on, the more he got mad and the more embarrassed I felt for the both of us. I couldn't believe I hadn't taken the time to teach him how to hold the bat, much less swing it at a pitched ball!

After we left that first practice, my son was totally discouraged, telling me how horrible he thought he had done. I tried to encourage him, but to be totally honest, the first few practices of the season were awful. We kept going back to practice, and the same results kept happening. Landon simply could not hit the baseball, and the longer it went on, the more frustrated he got about the baseball season.

One night on the way to practice, my son said to me, "Dad, I'm a terrible hitter." I thought for a moment, and with a rush of dad courage, I told him, "Landon, as long as you believe you're a terrible hitter you won't hit the ball. You need to start believing you can hit the ball." He looked at me more frustrated than before and said, "Whatever, Dad…"

Nothing really changed for Landon the next few weeks until finally one night he came home from a practice that changed everything. Apparently the coaches came up with a creative game called "King of the Hill" to help Landon and a few others get used to hitting the ball. During practice Landon finally started hitting balls and even smacked one or two into the outfield. When Landon came home you would have thought he had just won the World Series. He was ecstatic and yelling, "Dad, I hit the ball tonight!"

I was excited for him, but I knew the true test would come just a few days later at the Saturday morning game. Having played baseball before, I understood that hitting the ball in practice and hitting it when the pressure is on during a game are two totally different things. Game day arrived and I sat nervously in the stands watching. Because he hadn't hit the ball the entire season, Landon was the very last kid in the lineup. As with every at-bat for Landon, we prayed he would at least get walked so he could have the affirmation of running the bases and possibly scoring for the team.

As he walked to the plate, I was so nervous for him, desperately wanting him to succeed and hit the ball. I think all the other parents in the stands, including the parents on the other team, wanted Landon to hit the ball, and I started praying my standard prayer, "God help him hit the ball..." When he stood up to bat, his teammates began to chant, "KING OF THE HILL, KING OF THE HILL, KING OF THE HILL, KING OF THE HILL!"

SMACK. Landon hit the ball on the first throw! It went past the second baseman and rolled into the outfield as he ran to first base. He stood on that base as if he had just conquered the world and was beaming with excitement. All the parents and kids shouted wildly, "Good job Landon! Way to hit the ball!"

After that, everything began to change. He started to realize he could hit the ball, and for the whole rest of the season his demeanor and game changed dramatically.

### There were a few powerful things I learned about baseball that season:

1. Hitting the ball involves both the ability to swing the bat and the confidence to swing on time.

2. When you go up to bat without the confidence to hit the ball, you'll either hesitate and swing late, or not swing at all. Either way you can't hit the ball.

3. One major key to hitting the ball is believing you can hit the ball.

## God Wants us to Believe Rightly

The experience I had with my son revealed the power of what we believe and how it affects all of our actions. There is a powerful visual tool from Restoring the Foundations ministry, called the "Belief-Expectation Cycle."[3] This cycle shows that our life experiences can shape our beliefs, and in turn create expectations that determine our behavior. As a result of that behavior, we very often experience the fruit of that behavior which then validates our belief. This cycle can work for good or bad.

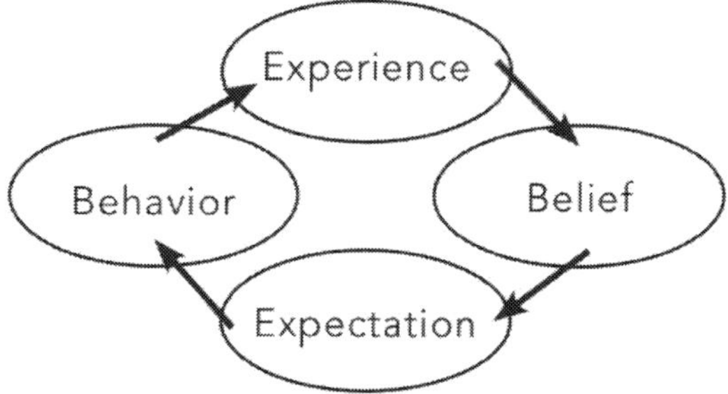


For example, in Landon's case, when he first started the little league baseball season, he believed he was able to hit the ball. All of his experiences from T-Ball told him that he was an amazing hitter. However, a new belief formed as he experienced not hitting the baseball in little league. Each time he didn't hit the ball, it would validate the belief that he was a terrible hitter, so when he stood up to bat he expected that he wouldn't hit the ball. His behavior would follow accordingly, and most of the time, he wouldn't even swing the bat because he didn't expect to hit the ball. The experience of not hitting the ball also reinforced the belief he had that he couldn't hit the ball. This downward cycle of belief can prove to be

---

[3] Klystra, Chester, and Betsy Klystra. Restoring the Foundations: an Integrated Approach to Healing Ministry. Proclaiming His Word Publications, 2001. Page 163

destructive in every area of our lives.

It wasn't until Landon had a new experience that he began to believe differently. When he finally played "King of the Hill" in practice and realized that he actually could hit the ball, he started to believe it. The more he hit the ball in practice, the more he believed. The more he started to believe, the more he hit the ball, and a new cycle of belief began.

The real test came during his first game. As he walked up to the plate, the battle warring within him, it was easy to forget what happened that last practice and revert to the old belief that he couldn't hit the ball. Thankfully his teammates started shouting to him a reminder that he *could* hit the ball. When they shouted, "King of the Hill," it translated into Landon's mind, "Remember, you can hit the ball!"

When he stood up to the plate remembering that he could hit the ball and believing that he would, he mustered up the courage to finally swing the bat and hit it. It was having the right belief that empowered him with the courage to hit the ball.

In my own personal journey, God has shown me over and over again how much more He wants to transform how I believe, rather than how I behave. It's my tendency to focus on my good or bad behavior and try to make my own personal adjustments. However, God knows that my behavior will never truly change until my heart and beliefs change.

## Change our beliefs then our behavior follows...

Behavior modification is temporary, but when we allow God to renew our minds as Paul encourages us in Romans 12, then everything else will change. It reminds me of drivers on an interstate. Most typically drive 5-10 mph over the speed limit until they see a highway patrolman on the side of the highway. Suddenly every car slows down in unison. Then, as everyone passes the officer and sees that the officer has faded from view, in perfect unison once again they resume their previous speed. This is what our lives look like when we simply focus on behavior modification and not on dealing with the deeper issue of what we believe.

In 2009, I went through a ministry program called Teen Challenge because of my battles with drugs and alcohol addiction. I went into the program in order to stop doing drugs. What I quickly realized is that God wasn't after changing my behavior, he wanted to transform my heart! He showed me over and over again that my bad behavior and addictions were all simply the fruit of poor beliefs I had about God and myself. It was there that God started me on the journey in discovering who He really is, and who He says I am. That journey continues even today.

The beautiful thing about the gospel is that when we put our faith in Jesus, we can receive the incredible blessings of entering into the New Covenant with Him. In this covenant, we surrender our lives to Him and He gives us new hearts and a whole new identity (Jeremiah 31:31). We go from finding our identity in our successes, our failures, and everything in between, to discovering that we are defined in an entirely new way when we are in Christ. We go from being slaves of sin to sons and daughters of a Holy God. Our identity is transformed when we come to Jesus and so is the way we live our lives.

We were created by God to live in relationship with Him and to partner with Him to display His goodness to all of the earth. When sin came into our lives, we were separated from our relationship with God and ultimately lost sight of who He really is. Sin also pulled us away from our originally intended missional purpose and left us wandering aimlessly towards vain pursuits and temporary successes. Jesus came to deliver us from the power of sin and grant us the power of the Holy Spirit. With the Holy Spirit, we are made new in every way. We are born again. Through the empowerment of the Holy Spirit and by the work of the cross, we are restored back into what we were created for and experience the joy that intimately knowing God brings. This is amazing news!

It's important for all of us to know that it's only through Christ that we can really know who God is and who we really are. Without the work of the cross, we are ultimately separated from God and ignorant of His goodness. Without accepting what Christ has done, we wander toward things that seemingly fulfill us and have the illusion of satisfying that gnawing ache in us all for our lives to have true purpose. It's only in Him that we discover who God is and who we are. When we begin this journey of knowing God and representing Him, we start to partake of a joy that is other-worldly – the kind of joy that transcends circumstances.

One of the greatest keys to accessing true joy in our lives is to be anchored in the truth of who God is, what He is like, and who we are in relationship to Him. These three simple truths can bring tremendous liberation. So much of our frustration and anxiety in life can be traced back to having a misunderstanding in one of these three areas.

It's important to know that apart from covenantal oneness with Jesus Christ, we cannot claim the benefits of having a new identity in Christ. When we are born again, through grace and by our faith, we are adopted into the family of God and receive a new inheritance and identity. Some people, however, struggle with knowing whether or not they have received the salvation and adoption that comes through Jesus Christ. If you struggle with this, I want to encourage you that the scriptures make it very clear how we can know we are born again and have received this new Identity in Christ.

Recently, a friend shared with me over coffee that we can look to the book of 1 John to know that someone has been born again. I have found these scriptures to be a helpful guide for myself and others. Below is a brief overview of six evidences of true salvation and a relationship with God.

## Six evidences of a new life in Christ:

1. A lifestyle of obedience toward God and His commands. 1 John 2:3-6
2. A confession of Jesus as the Son of God. 1 John 2:22-23
3. A response to sin that involves ongoing repentance and transformation. 1 John 3:6-10
4. The correction and discipline of the Father at work. 1 Jn 3:1-2
5. A genuine love toward other believers. 1 John 3:14
6. A life marked with the presence of Holy Spirit. 1 John 4:13

I would encourage you to meditate on each of these scriptures from 1 John. If you can attest to all of these things in your life, then you can walk in the assurance that you have been born again!

So many people struggle with the lie that they are not good enough or they haven't done enough to be saved. It's important that we settle in our hearts whether or not we have truly been born again. God doesn't want us to live in uncertainty and concern over our salvation!

If you find after reading the signs that you have not truly experienced salvation and the freedom that follows, I encourage you to receive the free gift of a new life in Christ right now by simply putting your faith in Jesus and what He did for you on the cross.

## Whoever God is to you, He will be through you.

Jesus said, "you shall know the truth (beliefs) and the truth shall make you free (behavior)..." (John 8:32). The more we allow God to reveal truth and transform our ungodly beliefs, the more we live like He intended. There is such joy and liberation that can be found in discovering the truth and allowing it to change the way we think. We can discover true joy when we start to see God for who He really is and who we are in relationship to Him.

From that place of understanding, we then discover that we can have a life that represents God well to the world around us. He has created us to be light and to shine brightly. When we step into this God-given purpose, then we experience a joy that is incomparable. We were created to display Him to the world around us! That's why He originally created us in His image and commissioned us to go and be fruitful and multiply. (Genesis 1-3)

Our primary purpose is to love Him first and to glorify God and to represent Him everywhere we go. So many people who have put their faith in Christ experience a lack of joy because they go no further than belief. It's when we put feet to our faith and start to step out that we find fulfillment in partnering with God in His work to redeem every nation, tribe and tongue.

## Barriers That Hold us Back

One of our greatest barriers is having a poor understanding of

God's character and nature. The best way to overcome this lack of understanding is to prayerfully study the Word of God and grow to know Him in prayer. When we begin to discover who God is through His word and prayer, then we can begin to truly represent Him well.

If we have an imbalance in understanding of God's nature or character, then we can have a tendency to represent Him poorly. If we view God as distant and angry, then we will represent Him that way to others. Also, if we believe that God is unconcerned about our lives, we can demonstrate that misunderstanding through our own apathy toward engaging others with the gospel and demonstrating the Kingdom of God.

Not only is our view of God significant, we also need to see ourselves correctly. One of the greatest barriers people face that keeps them from sharing the gospel with others is a faulty understanding of who they are. When we don't allow God to define our identity, worth and value, then we must find it somewhere else. Many times we drift off into the temptation of allowing others' view of us to define our value.

Allowing others to define our worth and value can be a seemingly good idea, especially when we are doing well and what others want us to do. It can start to affect us negatively, however, when we fall short of others' expectations and let them down. Allowing others to define our identity and significance is called the "fear of man." The fear of man is a roller coaster ride that many Christ-followers are still on today, going up with the approval and praise of others and down with break-neck speed when faced with disapproval and criticism.

When we live bound to the praises of others, one of our greatest fears will be to let others down or to have people dislike us. This drives us to not live out our missional calling because we know that if we share the gospel, we may be rejected. For those whose identity is defined by the people around them, rejection is their greatest fear.

The liberating reality of knowing our identity in Christ is that we are set free from the fear of man and can walk only in the fear of the Lord. We can then obey the Holy Spirit, step out in faith, and share the gospel with others, representing Him well wherever we go!

## Parable of the Last Son

One of the most familiar of all Jesus' parables is in Luke 15, when Jesus tells the story of two sons and a father. Many people refer to this parable as the "parable of the lost son" or "parable of the prodigal son." By giving the parable this title, it's basically stating that the main point is about the lost son leaving and then coming home. While I believe that the story is very much about the lost son coming home, I believe the story is equally as much about the son who stayed home.

Let's look at the context of the Luke 15 parable so that we can understand the purpose and the message. Jesus actually tells three parables that all are similar in purpose and are all directed to the same group of people.

Luke gives us the context in the first two verses of the chapter:

*"Tax collectors and other notorious sinners often came to listen to Jesus teach. This made the Pharisees and teachers of religious law complain that he was associating with such sinful people—even eating with them!" (Luke 15:1-2 NLT).*

Here we are given a lot of insight into the moment when Jesus began telling these parables. There were two distinct crowds sitting and listening intently to Jesus talk, but with very different motivations. The fact that both were listening gives us insight into why Jesus probably chose to share these specific parables at this particular moment. One very important detail is that Luke included the fact that the religious leaders were grumbling about how Jesus was eating and spending time with the "sinners". This is important because I believe it shows that all three of these parables are in response to what the religious leaders were saying. I believe Holy Spirit led Luke to include this contextual detail to give us insight as to why Jesus would choose the parables he was about to share.

All three of the parables were about giving both sides an

accurate understanding of God. Jesus knew that the major issue the sinners and the religious leaders were dealing with was an incomplete view of the Father. He told these parables with a heart exploding with love, hoping that they would both catch a true glimpse of the Father's character. He wanted them to believe correctly because he knew that one simple adjustment in their perspective could change everything.

Jesus did want the "sinners" to know that the Father loved them and was looking for them. At the same time, He was addressing the religious leaders' remarks.

In the final parable that Jesus shares with the crowd, He tells a powerful story of two sons and a loving father. The first son takes his inheritance early and goes off and squanders it with reckless living. This son loses everything and decides to go back home and ask to be a servant in his father's house. As he's walking home, practicing his apology, his father sees him from a long way off and abandons everything to run to him. The father, who represents God the Father in this parable, receives his son back and gives him a robe, a ring, and a pair of sandals.

At the end of the parable, Jesus really begins to get to the point. Like any good communicator, He saves the best and most powerful point for last. Everything he said previously was merely building momentum in order to drive his point home. Jesus wanted to reveal the true nature of the son's father and expose the hearts of the religious leaders.

Let's look to the end of the parable to see how Jesus is carefully revealing the nature of the Father:

*"Now his older son was in the field; as he came near the house, he heard music and dancing.*

*"So he summoned one of the servants, questioning what these things meant. 'Your brother is here,' he told him, 'and your father has slaughtered the fattened calf because he has him back safe and sound.'*

*"Then he became angry and didn't want to go in. So his father came out and pleaded with him.*

*"But he replied to his father, 'Look, I have been slaving many years for you, and I have never disobeyed your orders, yet you never gave me a goat so that I could celebrate with my friends. 'But when this son of yours came, who has devoured your assets with prostitutes, you slaughtered the fattened calf for him.'*

*"'Son,' he said to him, 'you are always with me, and everything I have is yours.'"*

*(Luk 15:25-31 CSB)*

Jesus waits until the end of the parable to introduce the other son who was working out in the field. When this son finds out that his brother had come home, he's furious and doesn't want to celebrate. He despised the other son because of how he had left the family and squandered everything.

Much is revealed when the son says to his father, "I have been slaving many years for you…" This son believed he was a slave in spite of the fact that he was a son. His misunderstanding about the father and about his own identity actually robbed him from living in the fullness that was available to him. We find this out when his father responds, "Son, you are always with me, and all that is mine is yours." The whole time this son could have had all the privileges of being a son, but because he believed he was a slave, he lived as one. The issue wasn't the father or his ability to provide, it was in the way this son viewed himself and his father.

## Three Simple Truths That can Change Everything

There are three truths that we can pull from the father's response in this story that we want to be sure we don't miss. Though they are simple, these three truths have the power to change every area of our lives!

"'Son,' he said to him,' you are always with me, and everything I have is yours.'" (Luk 15:31 CSB)

### Truth #1 - We are free to live as God's children, no longer slaves to sin and death!

The first thing the Father says is the word "son." I believe that this simple, but powerful statement was to remind him of who he really was. Rather than a slave, the Father wanted him to remember that his identity was that of a son. There is a major difference in a household between someone whose identity is a slave versus a son. A son has access to the father and his resources. The position of a son versus a slave is so vastly different, they can't even be compared or confused. You are either a slave, or you are a son.

**Take away from truth #1** - God wants us to know who we are as sons and daughters because this simple revelation of who we are in relation to Him can change everything. He wants to seal the truth of our sonship upon our hearts so that we will live from that reality and experience all that He has for us.

**Example:** Imagine living a life where you have always dreamed of visiting a particular theme park. You've spent so much time hoping to go there and thinking about all of the incredible things you would do there. You have never gone there, however, because you never had the money to pay the entrance fee. Then you find out the whole time that the park was actually owned by your father and your whole family has free access. When you finally realize who you are, then you get to take advantage of the benefits of having that position or identity. You get to go to your dream theme park whenever you want! So many people don't realize their position in Christ and therefore miss out on so much of what God wants them to experience in life.

## Truth #2 - We can be bold because we have access to God's presence at all times!

The second thing the father says in response to the son is, "you are always with me." This statement was very intentional. Jesus wanted to express the value and importance of living with an awareness of God's presence.

One of the most amazing realities of being a son or daughter of God is that we have free access to His person. We can remain in His presence! Because of the blood of Jesus, our sin and all that has separated us from God has been removed. We can now come boldly before Him as our "Abba" or "Daddy." When we understand the fact that He is always with us, we can be liberated from intimidation and fear. We can begin to face impossible situations with great boldness because we know that our Father, the creator of the universe, is right there with us.

**Take away from truth #2** - The degree to which we are aware of His presence in our lives will dictate the amount of courage and boldness we have to step into the destiny He's calling us to, and we can't do the incredible things He has called us to do *unless* He goes with us. We have the promise that He is *always* with us and we can count on His presence.

**Example:** Many times I've had the Holy Spirit direct me to stop and pray for someone or help someone with a seemingly impossible situation. When I look at the situation or the person and think of what I can possibly do for them, many times I want to run in the opposite direction! However, when I am aware of God's abiding presence, I'm willing to face the situation without fear or intimidation. I can be bold, knowing that the Creator of all things is coming with me!

## Truth #3 - We can be generous because we have access to the Father's resources!

The last thing that the father says has probably been the hardest for me to grasp and live out in my own life. He says to the son, "all that is mine is yours."

I want to encourage you to just take a second and think about the reality that you have access to everything that the Father has. If you look up the word "all" in the greek you will find the word "pas," which means "all." All means all. We have access to everything that is His. This astounding truth about His nature and the reality of our access according to our identity can transform everything. When we realize that God is our provider, that He will take good care of us, then we are empowered to take on His generous nature. We will be more likely obey the Holy Spirit when He prompts us to buy the groceries of the lady in line in front of us because we know He's our provider. We'll give generously of our time and belongings when we truly believe that everything that is His is also ours. This revelation of God's provision is one of the most foundational truths to discovering the joy of representing Christ in our everyday lives.

**Take away from truth #3** - In order for us to accurately represent Jesus, we must present to others a nature and behavior that is similar to His. One of the most powerful attributes about Jesus was the radical love expressed in laying down His life for us. His was the most clear depiction of generosity that the world has ever seen. When we realize our identity and how faithful our Father is to provide, we can begin to become generous as Jesus was generous.

## The Power of Generosity at a Subway

One day, as I made a hurried stop into a local Subway restaurant, I was waiting in an annoyingly long line when I sensed that the Holy Spirit was trying to get my attention. He started to quietly speak to my heart about the woman behind me. As I listened, I started to think that He wanted me to buy this woman's food. The more He made that clear, the more I resisted the idea. All kinds of excuses started coming into my mind. "What will others think?" "What if she's offended by my offer?" "Don't I need the money I'd spend on her for myself?"

The closer I got to the counter the more annoyed and nervous I got. Finally, I ordered my sandwich and as I'm about to pay I kind of reluctantly look at the woman behind me and ask her something like, "Can I buy your meal today?" Not only was she shocked, but the person at the register was kind of taken aback at the breach in social protocol. As soon as I obeyed the Lord, I sensed something had changed in that whole long line of people. The fragrance of Jesus Christ was released as I submitted my pride and stinginess to simply obey the leading of Holy Spirit.

After buying the sandwich for this woman she followed me over to the drink dispenser crying. She challenged me, "Why did you do that?" Unsure of what to say, I told her, "I just felt like God told me to do that." At that point she lost it and started to tell me her story. Several months before she was laid off at her job and hadn't been able to find another job. She woke up that morning to a house with no food left and walked to the Subway with her last 5 dollars to buy her last meal. She had no more money or food and didn't know what she was going to do. She was contemplating what to buy with the small amount of money she had when suddenly I looked at her and asked if I could pay for her order. When she told the story she was overwhelmed with the love of God and encountered the reality that God knew exactly what she was going through and heard her prayers. The last question she asked me was, "What church do you go to?" I smiled, told her, and then gave her a big hug.

## Final Thoughts on Discovering Identity

I've realized that the more accurately I know the nature of my Father and my position in relationship to Him, the more I will live as He has created me to live. He's made me in His image and has designed me to be His image bearer. My greatest enemy is not persecution or other people, but the lies I struggle with in my own head that prevent me from seeing the Father for who He really is. I am liberated from the fear of man and the pressure to perform when I realize that I have a radically generous Father who is always with me and is always going to take care of me.

The Father accepts us as His children not because of how good we are or how we perform, but because we are His delight. Nothing can ever change who we are to Him. We can be eternally His child and can live in the joy of knowing who we are in Him. Although God clearly does not condone or approve of our sinful behavior or lifestyles, we can know that when we come to Him in faith, we are accepted and loved, even before we ever make a change.

One of the most tangible ways that I've been able to grasp this has been in having my own children. When my kids are babies and toddlers and can't do anything at all for me, I am still proud of them and take pleasure in them. I enjoy them not for what they can do, but rather for who they are in relationship to me.

A friend of mine went through the long and expensive process of adopting a beautiful little girl who was abandoned by her parents. When she was officially adopted, everything changed from that day forward. Her name changed. Her citizenship changed. Her language changed. She went from unwanted and thrown away to wanted and the beloved of her new father. She became a forever part of a new family and nothing she ever did could change that. Her adoption was permanent and her destiny forever changed.

When we are adopted into the family of God, everything becomes brand new. We have a new destiny. We have a new position in life. We have a new hope and joy that otherwise would have never been possible. When we discover our new identity in Christ, we discover a joy that is incomparable. This entire book builds on this simple truth. Our discovery of joy begins with our discovery of who God is and who we are in relationship to Him.

Let's continue our journey...

# 3 - DISCOVERING CONNECTION

"Jesus never taught His disciples how to preach, only how to pray. To know how to speak to God is more than knowing how to speak to man. Power with God is the first thing, not power with men. Jesus loves to teach us how to pray."[4]
-Andrew Murray

I'll never forget the moment I was sitting at my desk at the Teen Challenge office with a baffling assignment in front of me. I was participating in a leadership training program that consisted of reading one book per month along with an assignment. I was enjoying the current book until I got to the assignment, which asked me to pray and write down what I believed to be my life's mission statement. The thought of attempting to identify my whole life's mission statement was overwhelming. Frustrated, I chose instead to tuck the notebook away.

After several weeks of procrastination, I pulled my notebook back out. Feeling a bit stumped because I still couldn't think of a concise statement for my whole life's purpose, I considered skipping over the assignment, but something in me was drawn to dig deeper into the idea of having a life's mission statement. Quietly praying at my desk, I began to hear the "still small voice" of God. I sensed God saying clearly to my heart "*Andrew, your whole life's mission is to abide in Me in such a way that you would inspire countless others to pursue Me with reckless abandon.*" I grabbed a pen and wrote it down.

Right then I discovered that my whole life's mission could be summarized simply in the word, "Abide." I knew God was telling me that if I would stay connected to Him, He could use my life in

4 Murray, Andrew. With Christ in the School of Prayer. Whitaker House, 2017.

great ways. My mission is not to do things *for* Him, but rather to stay so connected to Him that He could do things *through* me.

The more I have searched scripture and prayed over what God said to me that day, the more confirmation I have that ultimately my mission is to abide in Him. My mission isn't where I work or even what I do for God. My mission is to abide in Him wherever He calls me. When I do that I know that amazing things will happen in and through my life.

God can call us to start a business, go back to school, or become a janitor. No matter where we find ourselves, we can still fulfill this ultimate mission. If we remain connected to Him, no matter where He puts us, we can inspire others to want to know Jesus like we do. The closer we stay to Him, the more others around us will want to know Him too.

Discovering the joy of representing Jesus in our everyday lives is impossible if we're not staying connected to the source of our joy. We must stay connected to Jesus and get to know Him more if we want to accurately show who He is and what He's like to the world around us. When we abide in Jesus, our lives *will* have an eternal impact!

## Staying Connected to Jesus and His Body

*"I am the true vine, and my Father is the vinedresser. Every branch in me that does not bear fruit he takes away, and every branch that does bear fruit he prunes, that it may bear more fruit. Already you are clean because of the word that I have spoken to you. Abide in me, and I in you. As the branch cannot bear fruit by itself, unless it abides in the vine, neither can you, unless you abide in me. I am the vine; you are the branches. Whoever abides in me and I in him, he it is that bears much fruit, for apart from me you can do nothing."* (John 15:1-5 ESV)

For the longest time, I read John 15 in an individualistic manner. By that I mean that the picture I would have in my mind was Jesus as the vine and myself as my own branch. What I have discovered, though, is that John 15 is actually a call for us as individuals and *corporately* to be connected to Jesus.

The context of John 15 is a corporate invitation, not simply a conversation with an individual. He's talking here to a large audience, and the culture He is talking to is communal, not individualistic. When they heard Jesus saying these words, they wouldn't have thought about it in an individual manner, but rather in a communal one. He said in John 15:5, "*I am the vine and you (plural) are the branches (more than one).*" (Parentheses are mine.) When Jesus was speaking to them, they weren't just wondering how this affected each of them, they were thinking how it affected ALL of them.

Abiding in Jesus is a corporate invitation for *all of us* to stay connected to Jesus and to each other. The call to abide in Him cannot be separated from the call to live in oneness with those in the Body of Christ.

In order to stay connected to the vine, we must be connected to its branches as well. In the context of this scripture, He is inviting his audience collectively to stay connected to Him. This requires each individual to commit to stay connected to Jesus and to other branches that may be integral to their connection with Him.

This is made even more clear just two chapters later in John 17 when Jesus brings this conversation with the disciples to an end with a prayer. He prays that His disciples would be made one or be brought together in the same way that He and the Father are one. This request reveals the heart of God– that the family of God is working together in love, harmony and oneness.

## Three practical ways I believe we can stay connected to others:

1. Be a part of a thriving local church in your community. The local church is one of the primary ways we stay connected to Jesus and His Body.

2. Relate closely to other Christian friends. Consistently meet with people who know you well enough to be able to tell when you need encouragement or have the ability to challenge you when needed.

3. Get involved with others in ministry or business who have a

similar passion as you. These people might be seen by some as "competition," but they can honestly be some of our greatest encouragers. When we humbly connect to those who lead churches, ministries and businesses in our city, region and nation, we can grow and have a greater impact than if we are separated.

All three levels are vital and important to living a life of abiding in Jesus and staying connected to the branches of community.

One of the things that God has been showing me the past few years is the importance of Christian community. I grew up in church, but wandered into a life of addiction and partying. When I finally surrendered to God's will for my life in a Teen Challenge program at 21, I was introduced to the power of Christian community. I quickly realized, though, that it was not perfect. In fact, within a few months of coming to Christ, a primary mentor of mine was discovered to be doing drugs and living in a homosexual relationship. This was just the first of many experiences of moral failures and other wild situations I've experienced while living in community.

As a result, I discovered that I had to work through my own distrust of the church and Christian leaders. I believe God allowed me to experience so much my first year to keep me from making idols of leaders and to keep me clearly focused on knowing Jesus. As God has healed my heart and helped me to forgive, He has shown me the power of living in an authentic Christian community, and that living closely with others, all of whom are far from perfect, is actually an integral part of His will for my life... and yours.

As I've traveled the past few years, I've met many Christians who say that they love Jesus but just don't like church. In a lot of ways, I can understand what they are saying, but I always encourage people to be connected to the Church no matter how dysfunctional it might be. So many live under the illusion of an individualistic interpretation of scripture and see their spiritual journey as just a "me and God' type reality. The truth is that from the beginning, God makes it clear how important community is. In fact, the first thing He says about this is in Genesis 2:18: "It is not good for man to be alone." The wild thing about this statement is that Adam had unhindered access to creator God in the perfection of the Garden of Eden and yet God still said that wasn't enough. God knew that since man was created in His image, he also was in need of community. God is an expression of perfect harmony, union and community in the indescribable reality of the Trinity – Father, Son, and Holy Spirit.

Another common example used is the picture of us as the Body of Christ and Him as the head of that Body. If we are removed from the Head, that is Christ, we cannot live. Also, if we disconnect from other parts of the body we cannot live. If the arm disconnects from the shoulder then the arm will die. If the lungs disconnect from the heart, they will die. If a foot disconnects from the leg, then the foot will die (see 1 Corinthians 12).

Abiding in Christ looks like staying in intimate connection with Jesus himself and with our fellow branches. We must get rid of our individualistic lens and begin to understand that the invitation to abide is not for us alone but for us (the Body of Christ) as a whole. Holy Spirit wants us to see John 15 as an invitation to remain connected to Jesus and others who are also connected to Jesus.

Think of a fire and its embers as an analogy. The flames represent God (see Hebrews 12:29). Embers and coals represent Christians living in community and oneness together. If you remove a coal from the flame or other coals, it will burn out. It cannot survive without the flames' consuming energy. But, if you keep the coal in the fire and among other hot coals, it will keep burning.

## Liberated from Striving

One of the most liberating statements in the entire Bible is when Jesus said in John 15:5, "Apart from me you can do nothing." The truth of this verse liberates us from striving and straining to try and make things happen for God. Many times when we think of living for God and sharing the gospel, we think of all the things we need to do more– share the gospel more, go to church more, read and pray more. More and more activities, outreaches, and programs. The reality that we find in this scripture is that apart from Jesus, we can't do anything.

*"You did not choose me, but I chose you and appointed you so that you might go and bear fruit—fruit that will last—and so that whatever you ask in my name the Father will give you"* (John 15:16).

We didn't choose Jesus, Jesus chose us. We don't do things for God, rather we are appointed by God to go and bear fruit. Our calling is not to go and strive for God. We're simply called to stay connected to Jesus, lean into His grace, and allow Him to use us. Since He's the one who chose us, then we can trust that He will give us everything we need to be faithful to Him. We can allow Him to do all the heavy lifting while we simply focus on being connected to Him. We have nothing to prove.

So many times when I am struggling to abide in Jesus, or find myself entering into striving, it's connected to my own inability to live from my true identity in Christ. So much of striving comes from trying to prove something to God or to others. When I know that I am already valued and accepted by my Father in heaven, then I am liberated from constantly striving and can enter into the rest of abiding in His love. Knowing my identity in Christ is directly linked to my ability to be free.

This lesson of being liberated from striving, in my opinion, is not one that is ever fully realized. I believe that in our journey we're going to be consistently challenged to trust God and to choose not to strive. God calls us to do things that are bigger than we can even understand. Even when we feel like we've arrived and are truly trusting God, He'll ask us to do something new that is intimidating and scary.

When I first started Take the City, I did a city-wide outreach with a Teen Challenge leadership training conference with about 150 people in attendance. I had never done anything like it before, so I was overwhelmed, and had to trust God each and every day. When the teams arrived the day of the event, we had successfully mobilized 15 outreach groups of 10 people each to go out across our city sharing the gospel and meeting various needs. I was so elated to see God provide and help us do what was much bigger than I could have handled on my own.

About six months after this first event, we began discussing the next one. I started telling my team how excited I was for all that we were going to do. I knew this next year would be even better because we had all our planning documents created and the logistics figured out. All we needed to do was run with the plan we had used before. I was excited!

I'll never forget when someone made the suggestion, "Hey, instead of doing what we did last year, let's rent a huge venue and invite thousands of people to come hear the gospel!" Everyone on the call got really excited, except me. The other leaders on the call all started throwing out ideas, getting more and more excited. By the end of the call, I was again overwhelmed, and slightly irritated. I just wanted to go with the plan from the last year!

I agreed to make a phone call to appease the group and find out the cost of the venue. I procrastinated for at least two months. When I finally called right before the team met again, I was excited to find out that the venue had already been reserved for the dates we were hoping for. I was thankful and thought that I had gotten out of planning such a huge event until the woman from the city said, "Actually, you should call the group that has reserved the venue that weekend. They are a Christian group and you might be able to join up with them." When she said that, I grew a little uneasy, but agreed to call.

After I explained our ministry and idea to the woman from the Christian group, I realized she was crying. She told me that everything I had shared with her was exactly the same thing that they were planning and that it was as if I was reading their event planning sheet. From that moment, I knew the Lord was up to something!

Over the next four months, our groups joined forces and we planned our very first Revival on the River. I fought the temptation to strive and control the situation, and looking back, realize that God wanted this event to happen even more than we did. He guided us along the way even though each of us were totally unqualified to pull off such an event In less than 90 days, we had put together an event that hosted over 2,500 people. God even supernaturally connected us with Chick-fil-A, who agreed to feed everyone a free meal the night of the event!

As God continues to ask me to do things that are harder and more challenging than I can imagine, I learn to trust Him more and to let go of the temptation to make things happen in my own strength. I'm learning to lean more into the grace of God, stay close to Him, and allow Him to do the impossible. The result is a profound joy in the journey, an awe of seeing Him at work, and enjoying the privilege of partnering with Him. In doing so, the glory remains His alone.

## Being with Jesus

"*And they took note that these disciples had been with Jesus*" (Act 4:13).

God has put the desire in each of us for communion and relationship. This has become obvious in any public setting. Everywhere you look, you see people on their phones– connected to social media, on a call, or sending emails. All of these things can be good but they will never truly satisfy what we're longing for. These God given desires for connection can only be satisfied when we come to Jesus.

When we spend time with Jesus, others will take notice. Our time with Him causes our lives to make a true and lasting impact on others. We are called to represent Him well in our everyday lives and the only way we can do that is to know Him well by spending time with Him.

I've applied for many different jobs in my lifetime and most companies asked for the same thing– references. Each prospective employer would not only review my job history and life, but would call my references in order to really know who I am. They didn't just want the historical facts, they wanted to talk to someone who had actually spent time with me. Someone who had seen me at my best and at my worst and could truly ascribe to what kind of character and work ethic I possessed.

I believe that this same principle applies to our witness for Christ. People we encounter in our families, workplaces and everyday lives aren't just looking for the facts we know about God, they are looking for people who have actually gotten to *know* the God they are talking about. The importance of intimacy with God is paramount when it comes to representing Him accurately.

When it comes to job references, "How long have you known this person?" is a common question asked. This question is crucial, because time is important when it comes to familiarity with a person. The more time you've spent with someone, the more that person can vouch for who you are. It's also a critical factor when it comes to knowing Jesus and abiding in Him. I'm not saying that you can't be a good representative of Jesus until you have known Him for years, but I do believe that how much time we spend with Him each day helps us as we share Him with others around us.

When I take time to be with Jesus, I like to view it as I would spending time with anyone else. Sometimes, I want to spend hours with Him before my day starts. Other times, I may stop for 15 minutes in the middle of my day to be with Him. In the same way, I want to be with my wife and family in the morning, call them on my lunch break, and spend time together in the evening. To *abide* in Jesus means that I remain closely connected to Him, not just part of each day, but throughout each day. When the apostle Paul said we should "*pray without ceasing,*" he was encouraging us all to stay in constant communication with God.

*"...apart from me you can do nothing" (John 15:5b).*

When Jesus says that apart from abiding in Him we can do nothing, He's describing an unchanging reality that without staying connected to Him we really can't do anything that will have an eternal impact. This is a sobering fact. Everything I have done, good or bad, will ultimately have no lasting and eternal impact if it was done apart from Christ. I believe that even in full-time ministry, we can do good things, build buildings, have money and even a lot of followers, but ultimately not bear any eternal or lasting fruit.

When the work of our hands and the labor of our lives comes from our own ambitions or striving, it will ultimately fade away like everything else in this temporary world. Conversely, everything we do in response to our communion with Christ will remain forever. It's critical that in whatever we do, we do it from a position of knowing the Lord deeply.

I can't stand the feeling of pressure that comes when salespeople try to exert their will over mine to their own advantage. I've seen many evangelism and witnessing techniques that look very similar to a high pressure sales pitch. Many times these techniques have all the right scripture, great terminologies, and sound doctrine but are birthed out of the wrong heart posture.

When we try to represent Jesus and share the gospel with others in order to prove something or to gain more of God's approval, the people we are sharing with will likely feel like a "project" or the victim of a high pressure sales pitch. People can usually sense the real motivation behind our religious activities and our sharing of the gospel. When we do these things out of our own striving and ambitions, we can actually find ourselves misrepresenting Jesus. Even though we might be saying all the right words, the message can be convoluted by our misdirected motivation.

When we spend time with Jesus, He will begin to transform us more and more into His likeness. The more we are with Him and the more we become like Him, the better we will represent Him. When we're connected to Him, He will share His heart for people. From that place of knowing Jesus and His heart for others, we can then begin to share.

"*And we all, who with unveiled faces contemplate the Lord's glory, are being transformed into his image with ever-increasing glory, which comes from the Lord, who is the Spirit*" ( 2 Corinthians 3:18).

# 4 - DISCOVERING PURPOSE

From the very beginning, God created humanity full of destiny and purpose. He made you and me not only for the purpose of relationship with Him, but also that we might partner with Him to further His goodness and blessing upon the entire earth. God created the heavens and the earth in Genesis, and the Bible says that God, "saw all that He had made, and it was very good" (Gen 1:31 NIV).

From the very beginning, God's heart has been to demonstrate His goodness through His creation. When He made us in His image, we were made to express and carry that goodness to the ends of the earth. We were given an assignment, to "Be fruitful and increase in number; fill the earth and subdue it" (Gen 1:28 NIV).

However, everything changed when Adam and Eve were deceived by Satan and they started to doubt the character and goodness of God. They had been given a charge by God in the beginning to spread the goodness of the Garden of Eden until it covered the entire earth. We know from the scriptures that part of the planet was covered with a heavenly garden in which Adam and Eve lived and that the rest of the earth was not that way. We don't know what the rest of the world was like outside the garden, but we do know that God's desire was that the garden would extend to the far reaches of the earth.

We also know that God could have easily covered the earth with the garden by Himself, but instead chose to partner with humanity to fulfill His purpose and to express His goodness. Adam and Eve had been delegated authority from God to go and further this heavenly reality. When they disobeyed God, they entered into sin and rebellion. This not only caused death, but also caused them to be cast from the garden and derailed them from their intended purpose and destiny.

When they are cast out of the garden, we immediately see the beautiful plan of redemption begin. In the midst of God's plan, we also see that Satan is initiating a plan of his own and a war begins for the eternal destiny of all those on earth. Instead of mankind taking dominion over the earth, we forfeited what was ours to Satan, who then became the ruler of the earth. Satan hijacked the authority that was given to us and began his plan to "steal, kill and destroy" (John 10:10) as much as he possibly could. Thankfully, we know through the Word of God that the plans and the purposes of God for mankind could not be permanently derailed.

In Genesis 12, God made a covenant with Abram with the promise that through his descendants, He would bless the entire earth. He invited Abram into the original destiny and purpose of mankind through this covenant. According to Genesis 15:17, God was the only one who walked through the ritual to finalize that contract, which created a covenant that was purely by faith and through grace alone. The purpose of this covenant was to enable mankind to enter back into our God-given destiny to be a blessing to all of the earth.

God used Moses and the people of God to create a tabernacle, a sacred tent that the people of Israel constructed after their exodus from Egypt. This tent pointed the people of Israel back to the Garden of Eden and toward the inevitable future of God's heavenly Kingdom covering the earth. The tabernacle's symbols and various items that were a part of the design and construction intentionally served as a constant reminder of what once was in the Garden and what was to come. The tent was a picture of Israel's role in taking the reality of the Garden and extending it throughout the earth. The presence of God filled the tent and the people of Israel lived in a form of closeness to God, while He led them through the wilderness for forty years. Eventually, they were led by the ark of God's presence into the promised land where they took dominion and set up the tabernacle for worship until the Temple was constructed by King Solomon (see 2 Chronicles 3-5) as a resting place for the Ark of the Covenant.

As we continue to read through the scripture, we see that mankind continuously fell short of our destiny over and over again and that Satan was adamant that we would never fulfill our originally designed destiny. Israel was led astray by idolatry and false Gods over and over again. They were tempted to disobey God and to walk away from Him. They continued to go back and forth and eventually, it even appears that the biblical story starts to go backward when they end up again in captivity in Babylon. They had disobeyed God to the point that they had lost the land that God had promised them, yet it was through these people and that specific land that God promised He would bless the entire earth.

A ray of hope appears as God raises up the prophets during the time of Israel's captivity. They start to prophecy what God was saying: "I will make a new covenant with the house of Israel... I will put my law within them, and I will write it on their hearts. And I will be their God, and they shall be my people. I will forgive their iniquity, and I will remember their sin no more" (Jeremiah 31:31-33). These rays of hope point to the reality that God was going to do something totally new and remove the sin nature that had been keeping humanity from their ultimate potential and destiny.

When Jesus arrives on the scene in John 1-2, we see that John the Baptist calls Him the "Lamb of God that has come to take away the sins of the world." This beautiful introduction points to the reality that when Jesus came and died on the cross for our sins, He came to initiate a new covenant with His own blood. He's the lamb of God because He made the perfect sacrifice on our behalf to initiate this incredible new covenant. With the death, burial, and resurrection of Jesus, the reality of the new covenant was introduced, and for the first time, humanity was able to receive a new nature and a new heart. Through Jesus Christ, they were invited by God to throw off the old nature that was started with Adam and Eve's rebellion and to receive the precious Holy Spirit into their lives who would become the leader of their lives and change their nature. That same invitation is ours today.

With this new covenant, we can now enter back into our original destiny and purpose! Because of His blood, we can be washed clean and made totally new. Because of His blood, the curse that came from the garden is broken and we are liberated! When Jesus shed His blood, He defeated Satan once and for all, and by His blood and through our testimonies, we can now overcome Satan in the earth. As we love others, preach the gospel, heal the sick and demonstrate the Kingdom of God, we are living out the core of our intended purpose as image bearers of God.

From the beginning God's will and desire has always been the same. He has always had "as a plan for the fullness of time, to unite all things in Him, things in heaven and things on earth" (Ephesians 1:10). His purpose has been to take the reality of heaven and make the earth experience that same reality. The garden of Eden was a picture of heaven on earth. Adam and Eve were to extend the reach of this heavenly reality to the entire earth. When Jesus came as the second Adam, He reinstated us back into our original calling to bring heaven to earth. Jesus invited us all back into our original purpose when He invited us to pray, "Your kingdom come, your will be done, on earth as it is in heaven" (Matthew 6:10)

## Ambassadors for Christ

In 2 Corinthians 5 it says that we are now "ambassadors for Christ" and that we are given the "ministry of reconciliation." This chapter makes it clear that God is making His appeal through us to the rest of humanity to come back to God. When we become a disciple of Jesus Christ and are born again, we are invited back into the original plans of God for us to represent Him and to further his purposes on the earth. It's amazing to think that through Christ, God can take broken vessels like you and me, and bring redemption and hope to the entire earth. Let's take a closer look at the last half of 2 Corinthians 5:

*"Therefore, knowing the fear of the Lord, we persuade others. But what we are is known to God, and I hope it is known also to your conscience. We are not commending ourselves to you again but giving you cause to boast about us, so that you may be able to answer those who boast about outward appearance and not about what is in the heart. For if we are beside ourselves, it is for God; if we are in our right mind, it is for you" (2 Corinthians 5:11-13).*

Paul begins this section of the chapter with the word

"therefore," which points us to the previous part of the chapter where he was talking about "our life here on earth is temporary and we all will face eternity." In light of our eternal reality and the fact that the earth is not our real home, we are to give our lives to "persuade others" and share with them about the hope that we have found. Our eternal perspective should compel us to become ambassadors for Christ during our short time on the earth.

*"For the love of Christ controls us, because we have concluded this: that one has died for all, therefore all have died; and he died for all, that those who live might no longer live for themselves but for him who for their sake died and was raised" (2 Corinthians 5:14-15).*

Our call to represent Christ is to be fueled by God's love. His love is what is to compel and control our every action. When we live a life of love, then we will live a life no longer for ourselves, but rather for Christ. When we encounter the gospel, we are set free from our bondage to our selfish nature and we're invited into a life of love and selflessness. In the same way that Jesus gave up himself for others and stooped down for the lowest of the low, so are we to give up our lives to demonstrate God's love for others.

*"From now on, therefore, we regard no one according to the flesh. Even though we once regarded Christ according to the flesh, we regard him thus no longer. Therefore, if anyone is in Christ, he is a new creation. The old has passed away; behold, the new has come" (2 Corinthians 5:16-17).*

Through Christ, each one of us can become a new creation and receive a new identity. While we were all sinners and formerly at enmity with God, we are now adopted into His family and given the assignment to be ambassadors for Him everywhere we go (see Romans 5:10). This is one of the most amazing realities found in the Bible and is an indispensable part of the gospel message. We have been made totally new and now can represent Jesus everywhere we go without hindrance from our old sinful nature and past mistakes. Through the blood of Jesus we can be totally forgiven and commissioned to represent God everywhere we go!

*"All this is from God, who through Christ reconciled us to himself and gave us the ministry of reconciliation; that is, in Christ God was reconciling the world to himself, not counting their trespasses against them, and entrusting to us the*

*message of reconciliation" (2 Corinthians 5:18-19).*

We have all been given, by the Lord, a job to do or "ministry" to carry out. The book of Corinthians isn't just a letter addressing the pastors or worship leaders in the church of Corinth. This was a letter for everyone! Our calling as ambassadors is tied to this single mandate: That we help reconcile others back to the Father through Christ. We get to share the incredible news that, through Christ, we can all have our trespasses and sins removed and can be reconciled back into who we were originally created to be! Our message and assignment is not one of judgement and condemnation, but rather as ambassadors of hope, helping to reconcile humanity back to the Father.

*"Therefore, we are ambassadors for Christ, God making his appeal through us. We implore you on behalf of Christ, be reconciled to God. For our sake he made him to be sin who knew no sin, so that in him we might become the righteousness of God" (2 Corinthians 5:20-21)*

We are not only God's children, we are also His ambassadors. The astounding fact about this reality in Christ is that God is actually "making his appeal through us…" He has chosen each of us, through His son, by the power of the Holy Spirit, to represent Him to the rest of humanity. We have the privilege and honor to engage every person we meet on behalf of the God of creation. Imagine if we viewed every single interaction we had on a daily basis in this way. How much different would our lives look when lived with a constant reminder of this reality?

## Meeting a Real Life Ambassador

When I was around 20 years old, I remember meeting an ambassador for the first time. From the moment I met him, I was impressed. A kind, humble, and dignified man, I could tell he had spent his life with kings, presidents and leaders around the world. I could see it in the way he carried himself and the way he communicated with others. I remember asking him what he did, and was excited to hear that he served as an ambassador for the nation of Suriname in South America. He told us many stories about the experiences he'd had during his career and I loved hearing all that he had done around the world.

Ambassadors of nations serve a very important role for the country to which they are assigned. Because the leader of a country does not have time to traverse the whole world or meet with other nations all the time, they appoint ambassadors who can go and represent them. An ambassador is given a great measure of authority and power to represent the nation from which they come. They understand the heart, intentions and will of their leader so that they accurately represent their country.

When they travel to a foreign land and meet with other leaders, it's as if their own leader was there. When ambassadors meet at the United Nations to vote on decisions that will affect the globe, it is not the leaders of those nations who cast the vote, but their ambassadors and delegates on their behalf. Think about the weight of the privilege and responsibility that carries.

When Jesus commissioned us as His disciples and gave us His very authority (Matt. 28:18-19) He was essentially empowering us to be His ambassadors. He said that all authority had been given to Him and now he commissioned them, and us, to go.

In Acts 1:8, they are instructed to go and wait in Jerusalem because He was going to also give them power through the Holy Spirit to help them carry out the task. Jesus commissioned His disciples as ambassadors and gave them both the authority and the power that they needed to preach the message of the Kingdom of God to every nation. When we realize that we are ambassadors for Christ, we also  come to understand the great measure of authority that has been given to us by God Jesus has given us all we need to obey His command to go and give witness to the good news!

## Mall Cop

In the movie, *Paul Blart: Mall Cop*[5], there is a powerful demonstration of the importance of having authority and power.

In the beginning of the movie, it's revealed that Paul's lifelong dream was to be a police officer for his local city government. He's

5 Garner, Todd, et al. Paul Blart, Mall Cop.

always wanted to have the badge and serve his community, but he's never been able to pass the rigorous test required to be sworn in and given the badge of authority. He eventually settles for the lesser and becomes a mall cop instead.

Throughout the movie you can tell how badly Paul wishes he had the true authority of a police officer, but because he's a mall cop he really has no true authority at all. Over and over again, he tries to correct and stop people and they blatantly disregard him when they realize he doesn't have any true authority. In a scene where he's training a rookie mall cop, Paul shows him a stance he would frequently do to make people think he had a gun. In reality, he had no power to exercise any measure of force to stop anyone. He also tries to stop an older man for driving too fast on his electric scooter, but the man accelerates right past him when he realizes that Paul is no more than a mall cop. He had no real authority to carry out his duties and no real power to bring about any change.

The sad reality is that many Christ followers today live with a "mall cop" mentality. They don't realize that they have been given true authority & power to do the things Jesus has commissioned them to do. They believe that the gospel is just the fact that Jesus died so that they can go to heaven. This is a sad reality to live in and falls horribly short of the biblical standard we see in the early Church in the book of Acts! Jesus did not send his disciples out ill-equipped. He made sure they not only had the authority they needed to carry out the assignment, but also the power they needed to complete it!

When Jesus first was walking with his disciples, Luke 9 says that "He called the twelve together and gave them power and authority over all demons and to cure diseases, and He sent them out to proclaim the kingdom of God and to heal" (Luke 9:1-2).

When Jesus sent out His new ambassadors, they were not only equipped with the message of the Kingdom, but also the authority they needed to demonstrate the message. This was not only intended for the first disciples, but also for those who saw Jesus after the resurrection. He told those to whom He appeared, "you will receive power when the Holy Spirit has come upon you..."

(Acts 1:8). This promise in Acts 1 was pointing to the idea that Jesus wanted all of His disciples to walk in the power of the Holy Spirit so they could fulfill their assignment to "go into all the world and proclaim the gospel to the whole creation… these signs will accompany those who believe: in my name they will cast out demons;.. they will lay their hands on the sick, and they will recover" (Mar 16:15-18).

We have been given an assignment that we cannot do in our own power and our own authority. We don't have in ourselves what this world needs! Thankfully Jesus did not expect us to simply rely on our own measure of authority and power but has delegated His authority to us and, by the Holy Spirit, had distributed His power.

We've also been given the power of the Holy Spirit to validate our message. When we represent God everywhere we go, we can be assured that we have all of heaven backing us. We can be confident that we're not alone in our efforts, but that the Spirit of God desires to confirm the message of reconciliation by bringing conviction of sin, the healing of the sick and other displays of supernatural power. God wants us to not only know that we have great authority and power in the Kingdom of God, but He also invites us to use it for His glory and to expand His dominion in the earth.

There is a joy that is discovered when you partner with God in His will to use you as ambassadors for Him in the earth. When you say "yes" to your assignment, know your authority in the earth and the power you have in the Holy Spirit you can live a life of incomparable joy. You were created by God to represent Him where He has placed you. Whether you are a stay-at-home mom, working the corporate world or a pioneer missionary to unreached people, His desire is that you would represent Him.

As you grow in your knowledge of the power and authority that you've been given you will begin to experience greater measures of joy. You've been given the ministry of reconciliation. There's no greater joy than living a life that helps to reconcile lost sons and daughters into the family of God!

# 5 - DISCOVERING THE CALL

For me, being a witness and sharing the gospel didn't come naturally. I knew after I decided to follow Jesus that I needed to participate in the great commission and make disciples but honestly, I didn't really want to or know how. It felt uncomfortable to share my testimony and talk to people about Jesus. Thankfully, over time, when I started to step out and take risks God began using me to lead others to Christ.

One of my first memories of being a witness was while traveling with a ministry team. We had stopped in a small midwest town and were relaxing in a coffee shop. I felt an urge to find some people to share Jesus with and we found out that there was a large population of homeless teens and young adults in that town. We went looking for anyone we could find and had the opportunity to spend several hours just sharing coffee and talking with them.

Nearing our time to go, I met a young couple and started telling them my story and what Jesus had done for me. I felt nervous steering the conversation to the topic of spirituality, but I realized that as I started sharing, Holy Spirit began to inspire and lead me. The more I shared, the more excited I became. I remember watching their response to the conviction of the Holy Spirit as they listened to me talk. Right there on the street, they heard my testimony about how God had delivered me from addiction to drugs. They responded to the simple gospel and put their faith in Jesus Christ. I got to lead them in making that commitment and encouraged them to find a local ministry where they could continue to grow.

What a feeling I had after leaving that situation! I felt so alive, more than I ever had before. I felt filled with indescribable joy. As I shared my testimony and led this homeless couple to Christ, something inside of me came to life. From that experience, I began to realize that I was created to not only experience the goodness of God for myself, but was also made to invite others to know Him.

Over the next few years, God really started to pull me out of my shell. I would have seasons where God would use me extraordinarily and then other seasons where it seemed that I had lost my touch to minister to others. I continued to grow in my relationship with Jesus and the more I fell in love with Him, the more I wanted others to come to know Him. The more I encountered His love, the more I wanted to share it with others. I discovered that the key to living an outward focused, missional lifestyle is staying connected to Jesus.

When others meet me through my ministry, most are surprised to learn that I am an introvert by nature. This means that God has created me in a way that I recharge best by being alone. I enjoy solitude. I love having a day to just be alone, read, work outside, run, write, etc… For me, sharing the gospel with others and being a witness isn't the result of a natural personality bent, rather it's the working of the Holy Spirit in my life. I've also realized that God actually wants to use me to reach others just the way He created me. He doesn't want me to strive to become anything He hasn't already made me to be. At the same time, it does require me to get outside of my comfort zone on a daily basis.

God wants to use my personality, my interests, experiences and travels, language, nationality, story and background all for His glory. He isn't hoping for me to become like some famous preacher or YouTube evangelist in order to reach others for Christ. He just wants my simple obedience to the calling we all have as followers of Jesus to go and be witnesses.

## 3 Keys to Living a life as a Witness: IDENTITY, POWER, PURITY

Over time I've discovered through my own personal story that there are three primary hindrances to living a life full of joy and representing Jesus everywhere I go. I want to share these obstacles and three keys that have helped me to share my faith more often.

## 1. Identity Leads to Destiny

*"But you are A CHOSEN RACE, A royal PRIESTHOOD, A HOLY NATION, A PEOPLE FOR [God's] OWN POSSESSION, so that you may proclaim the excellencies of Him who has called you out of darkness into His marvelous light" (1 Peter 2:9 NASB emphasis mine).*

As I mentioned in the first chapter, the key to living a lifestyle of evangelism and disciple making is directly connected to our ability to know and walk in our identity in Christ. In coming into our identity, we can serve our true purpose and live out our God given destiny. We have been given a new identity in Christ, "so that you may proclaim..." There is a purpose in God showing us who we are! It's so we can be empowered to share the good news of the gospel with others.

I've seen in my own life that the more I grow into my identity in Christ, the more I step into my calling to represent Jesus everywhere I go. When I know who He has created me to be, I can overcome the fear of man, the fear of failure and can live empowered and emboldened to be a witness.

Understanding our identity doesn't begin by looking at ourselves, but rather looking at the awesome and Holy God whom we serve. When we allow God to give us greater revelation and understanding of Jesus each day, we can grow in the understanding of who we are in relationship to Him. Don't be focused on yourself, but keep your eyes on Jesus and He will continually lead you to grow in knowing your own identity in Him!

## 2. Power from the Holy Spirit to Overcome Fear and Boldly Proclaim

*"You will receive power when the Holy Spirit has come upon you; and you shall be My witnesses…" (Acts 1:8 NASB).*

We can't live a life with boldness unless we have the power of the Holy Spirit leading us and compelling us. When I received what the bible calls the baptism of the Holy Spirit in 2011, my life began to radically change. One of the things that started happening after that encounter was that I became more bold in proclaiming the Good News. I had been following Jesus up until that point, but seemed to lack the boldness I needed to be able to step out and be a witness. I struggled through so much timidity and apathy. When the Holy Spirit filled me, I began to feel the way He did about those who were around me. I suddenly had this burning passion to share with others.

I'll never forget standing in a small Assembly of God church in the hills of Tennessee early one Sunday morning. I was tired and wasn't too excited to be in the church that morning with a group of guys from the Teen Challenge program. The pastor invited us all to pray together before the service. As we started, the pastor came over and put his hands on my head and began to pray. I suddenly felt a warmth all over my body and a surge of energy unlike I had never experienced before. A few moments later, I came back into consciousness and realized that I had literally been knocked to my seat and was speaking in a language I didn't understand. The first thought in my mind was, "I can't believe this is happening to me, I don't believe this is real!" It was a very real experience with a very real result. It was explained to me that I had been baptized in the Holy Spirit and the result was that my whole life was thrusted into a new level of faith, trust, and obedience to Christ. The very next week I started a journey of spending hours in prayer each day that lasted through the rest of that year. I began to share my faith and overcame hidden sin that I never thought I would be able to get past.

Up until that point, I was not open to "charismatic" experiences or pentecostal churches. I had been to many different local churches during my time with Teen Challenge and had seen some strange stuff. I wasn't sure that any of what I saw in the pentecostal churches was real. I was skeptical and would even mock some of the things I saw. Growing up, my church background was very traditional, so I wasn't readily open to the idea of the Holy Spirit actually encountering me in a real and authentic way. From the time I was baptized in the Holy Spirit, I have become much more open to the working of the Holy Spirit in my life and in others around me.

Many people may wonder why the baptism of the Holy Spirit is necessary. Don't we all receive the Holy Spirit when we are born again? The answer to that question is yes. The reality though, is that we are invited by faith to also receive an authentic encounter with the Holy Spirit that will empower us to not only boldly proclaim this message, but to live pure lives. John Piper, when speaking on the Baptism of the Holy Spirit, said, "the baptism in the Holy Spirit is more than a subconscious divine act of regeneration — it is a conscious experience of *power*."[6]

If you have never received the baptism of the Holy Spirit, then I would encourage you to stop reading for a moment and with faith pray this simple prayer: **"God, I want everything that You have for me. I need Your power and Your help. Fill me with the Holy Spirit that Jesus promised those who believe. I want more of You. Come and fill me and make me more like You. In Jesus name, Amen."**

Jesus made it clear just before his ascension that the baptism of the Holy Spirit was a special gift. He told his disciples to wait in the city of Jerusalem until they had received this special gift that was sent by God the Father to the early Church. Everything changed for the early church when they were baptized in the Holy Spirit.

*"And while staying with them he ordered them not to depart from Jerusalem, but to wait for the promise of the Father, which, he said, "you heard from me; for John baptized with water, but you will be baptized with the Holy Spirit not many days from now." (Act 1:4-5)*

## 3. Purity Removes the Obstacle of Hidden Sin and Shame

*"Therefore there is now no condemnation for those who are in Christ Jesus. For the law of the Spirit of life in Christ Jesus has set you free from the law of sin and death. For what the Law could not do, weak as it was through the flesh, God [did:] sending His own Son in the likeness of sinful flesh and [as an offering] for sin, He condemned sin in the flesh, so that the requirement of the Law might be fulfilled in us, who do not walk according to the flesh but according to the Spirit" (Romans 8:1-4 NASB).*

One of the greatest obstacles for many people in sharing the gospel with others is hidden sin. So many struggle with a life filled

---

6 https://www.desiringgod.org/messages/how-to-receive-the-gift-of-the-holy-spirit

with compromise and yet are still faithfully attending church and living a "good" life. The problem is that this often keeps people silent and from stepping into their calling to be a witness for Christ.

Thankfully, each one of us can access the powerful blood of Jesus to receive total freedom from all guilt, shame and condemnation. Through the power of the Holy Spirit we can live a life that overcomes the power of our sin nature. We have access to the same Holy Spirit that raised Jesus from the dead! If the Holy Spirit is more powerful than death itself, then how much more can we expect His working in our lives to help us overcome every area of sin and compromise.

*Every* person has fallen short and has made mistakes. Jesus lived a perfect life so that we can be totally forgiven. The amazing reality of what Jesus paid for on the cross is that we're not only forgiven, but are also redeemed to step back into our original purpose. God's not looking for perfection, but He is looking for those who are willing to set themselves apart, remove all hindrances, and live a life worthy of the calling of Christ.

Many times people want to live a life that makes an impact for the kingdom of God, but are unwilling to fully surrender and live a life of obedience. We see this with the story of the rich young ruler in Mark 10. This man wanted the benefits of the kingdom, but was unwilling to fully surrender to the King. Jesus is not only looking for our worship, but also for our obedience. This obedience is a choice of our will and is fully realized when we receive His empowering grace.

When we allow the Holy Spirit to work in us we can begin the journey to a life of purity and holiness. He wants to get rid of any junk that may be hindering us and our witness to others.

If there's something that has been getting in your way and has caused you to stumble into sin, take a moment to ask God for His forgiveness and receive His grace to live a life of victory. Take a moment to pray right now and ask the Lord to remove any guilt and shame, as well as anything that hinders you from loving others. He will help you to live a life of freedom by the Holy Spirit.

Also, it's important to remember that the Holy Spirit also works in our lives in the context of Christian community. It's important that we're connected to the Body of Christ and other people that can help us, hold us accountable and walk with us through our struggles. This is a huge key to having lasting freedom from sin and setbacks that keep us from being a bold witness for Christ.

## God's Strategy - "You will be my Witnesses"

"*So when they had come together, they asked him, 'Lord, will you at this time restore the kingdom to Israel?' He said to them, 'It is not for you to know times or seasons that the Father has fixed by his own authority. But you will receive power when the Holy Spirit has come upon you, and you will be my witnesses in Jerusalem and in all Judea and Samaria, and to the end of the earth*'" (Acts 1:6-8).

After Jesus' resurrection, the Bible says that He appeared to many and taught them until He ascended to be with the Father. Written by Luke, the ascension is recorded in Acts 1 and is one of those many moments in the scriptures where I wish I could have been there. One of the interesting things about this passage is that only one question is recorded. I've often thought that when Jesus was still walking on the earth, in the flesh, after the Resurrection, that I would have had a lot of questions for Him! I believe that this one question the disciples asked was of utmost importance.

Jesus came as the fulfillment of prophecies that were given over thousands of years. For generations, the people of Israel had been waiting for a promised "messiah" or "anointed one" that would be their king. They knew "that all the peoples, nations and men of every language might serve Him" and that "His dominion is an everlasting dominion which will not pass away." Their expectation of this Messiah is that He would lead Israel to have a kingdom that would literally rule the world, as well as being an "everlasting dominion," or in other words, a kingdom that never ended.

When Jesus died on the cross, all of His disciples were distraught and puzzled, wondering how someone who was dead could lead a kingdom that never ends. They knew Jesus said over and over that He must suffer and die, but they couldn't get past the ancient prophetic words from Psalms, Chronicles, Samuel and other places in the Old Testament (see 1 Chronicles 22:10, Psalm 45:6, 2 Samuel 7:13). One of the most overlooked parts of the gospel story for the gentile Church is that the Resurrection was the seal that proved that Jesus was the Messiah. The fact that Jesus defeated death and would live forever was the pinnacle of proof that was needed to show He was in fact their long-awaited Messiah. When the disciples saw that Jesus had been raised from the dead, they now knew without a shadow of doubt that He was the promised anointed King they had been waiting for!

The reason the question recorded in Acts 1:6 regarding the kingdom being restored is so important, is that in answering, Jesus gives us a clue as to how He wants to establish His kingdom during this present time in history. It was a strategy that the early disciples never would have thought of on their own. When they asked Him about the restoration of the kingdom to Israel, they were waiting for Jesus to tell them to rally the troops and start a global campaign to take over the world. They were thinking in human terms. Jesus doesn't correct them or even say that they were wrong for asking. Instead, He gives them a simple strategy for building God's Kingdom throughout the earth in this final season of history - they are to be His witnesses.

God's plan has not changed. One day we know that there will be a physical, heavenly kingdom that rules over the whole earth with Jesus as its king. Until that day comes, Jesus has commissioned us to join in His plan of building his kingdom, not with swords and spears, but with the power of the Holy Spirit. Rather than sending warriors with swords, He sent out witnesses and He is still sending us out today.

## What Does it Mean to be a Witness?

The word "witness" is translated from the greek word "*martys*." This word was a legal term that was used in a courtroom setting. When a person was on trial for a crime, they would call up a "martys" to share what they had seen, heard, or experienced. This greek word is actually where we get the modern English word "martyr." This is because most of those early witnesses for Christ were eventually killed for sharing their faith in various parts of the world.

This is a powerful word to study as it reminds us of what our job is and what our job is not. When we realize that we are called to be witnesses, our job is simply to share what we've experienced and how Jesus has changed our lives. Like a witness called to the stand in a courtroom, our job is not to convict anyone or to convince the judge or jury of anything. In the same way, as a witness for Christ, our job is to share and let the Holy Spirit do His job. We can feel relief from the pressure to perform and "get people saved." We can't save anyone. No one can come to the Father unless He's drawing them to himself. We can't make anyone want to know God, but we do have a mission to give witness anywhere and everywhere we go!

## What's a "Win" in Evangelism?

As a guy who grew up playing sports, I have a very competitive nature. Any time I start playing a game, I immediately want to figure out how to win. Even when I sit down with my family to play board games, I can't help but want to win the game!

When we look at evangelism, it is important that we ask ourselves the question, "What is a win?" How do we know when we have done a good job and how do we know when we haven't done well? Without knowing how to measure our success, we can't ever feel confident that we're obeying Jesus and doing what He's called us to do. God doesn't want us to be confused, He wants us to know what a "win" is!

Most people would think a win in evangelism is getting someone "saved" or "converted." I've travelled across the world helping churches to grow in impacting their communities for the gospel and have met countless people who believe that this is the true measure of success. The problem with this perspective is that often people act more like christian salespeople than witnesses for Christ.

## What's the Difference?

The success of a salesperson is rated by how many people say, "yes" to whatever they're trying to sell. When they sell something, it's a "win." When they don't, that's not a "win".

Conversely, the success of a courtroom witness is not determined by the conviction of the person on trial, but by whether they truthfully shared what they saw, heard and experienced. If they do that, then by the standard of any courtroom, they did an excellent job, or would in a sense "win."

When we have the revelation that we're not christian salespeople, but are called to give witness to what Jesus has done for us, we are liberated from striving and a performance mentality. So many people don't share their faith because they fear rejection and failure. Yet, we *can't* fail when we're sharing what He's done for us. We get a "win" every time we open our mouths and share the good news with others.

I love this quote I found from Billy Graham: "It is the Holy Spirit's job to convict, God's job to judge and my job to love."[7]

When I realize what is God's job and what is mine, I can live a life of freedom and joy! I don't have to put pressure on people or manipulate them. I don't have to feel a sense of failure when people reject the gospel. I can feel a sense of success and satisfaction when I am simply obeying Jesus' great commission. Whether someone responds with openness and wants to be born again or curses at me and tells me to leave them alone, I can be assured that if I shared the hope I've found in Jesus, I've done my job.

## Being a Witness at the Grocery Store

I'll never forget one of my first experiences taking a leap of faith and being a witness to a total stranger in public. Several years ago, I asked the Lord if He had anyone He wanted me to share with while at the grocery store. As I walked around, no one stood out until I got to the meat section. I felt that the Lord highlighted a woman to me and I tried to ignore it at first but the conviction became so strong that I knew I needed to go and talk to her about Jesus.

---

7 https://www.crosswalk.com/faith/spiritual-life/10-supernatural-ways-the-holy-spirit-wants-to-empower-you.html

I worked up the nerve to go speak to her, but still felt awkward as I approached. I also sensed God's love for her. As I started to tell her that Jesus loves her, she became outraged. She looked at me with utter disgust and started to yell and told me to get away from her. I was immediately overwhelmed and walked away. I remember feeling like a total failure and thinking, "God, did I miss You there?"

Later that night, I was at home and getting ready for bed. I started praying and asked the Lord about the experience earlier that day in the grocery store. I felt so rejected and hurt by the way the woman responded. I felt like I had failed.

As I started praying, I sensed the Lord begin to speak to me and encourage me. He made me realize that He was looking for my obedience and wanted me to trust Him with the results. He showed me that because of my willingness to share the love of Jesus, the Holy Spirit could use that moment to continue working in that woman's life, drawing her to the Father. He showed me that He could now begin to convict her and work in her heart to challenge her anger and the hurt she had experienced in the past. I realized that even though it appeared to be a failure, I had actually succeeded, *simply because I had obeyed.* It was now the Holy Spirit's job to convict her and draw her to Himself.

So many times we avoid situations like this, because it feels like failure. When we realize that obedience to Jesus is always a success, then we're more likely to step out in faith, share with others, and be bold in our witness!

## What is the Good News?

"*The Lord is not slow in keeping his promise, as some understand slowness. Instead he is patient with you, not wanting anyone to perish, but everyone to come to repentance*" (2 Pet 3:9 NIV).

The amazing reality of the gospel is the best news we could possibly ever share. There is no comparison to its transforming power. The gospel acts as a seed with limitless potential to transform not just individuals, but entire families, cities and nations.

God has given us this most powerful and incredible message to share with others!

I believe one of the reasons so many nations have suppressed the word of God and have tried to strip the Church of the right to share the gospel is because they are *afraid* of the power of this message. When the gospel message is preached, lives are changed and people are liberated. We serve a God who desires for each and every person to come to the saving knowledge of Jesus Christ!

## So what are the essentials of the gospel, or Good News?

First of all, the message is one of *love*. God so loved the whole world that He sent His Son, Jesus, to live a perfect life, die a death in our place, and defeat sin and death by the power of the Holy Spirit. Through what Jesus did for humanity, we're given an invitation and access to become sons and daughters of God. While in our sin, we were enemies of God, but through Jesus Christ we can become new creations and now be liberated from the power of sin and death! Without Jesus, we were destined for a life full of brokenness and ultimately an eternity in hell because of our sins, but Jesus came to restore our true destiny and give us a new life.

The simple gospel message can be summarized this way: Jesus came to this earth to restore us back into what we were created for. We were created, first of all, for relationship and communion with God Himself. Secondly, we were made by God with a mission and purpose to establish His goodness all over the earth. Our sin and mistakes not only separated us from God but also from being able to live out our true intended purpose. Jesus came to restore us back to God's original design, and will one day return to the earth to fully restore all things.

This message of the gospel is not just contained in what Jesus has done in the past but also in the promise of what He is coming to do. He is not only Savior of the world, but is also the soon coming King over all the earth. One day every knee will bow and every tongue will confess that Jesus Christ is Lord. One day, all the earth will be eternally liberated by the oppression of darkness and sin and will be ruled by a King with absolutely no compromise or flaws. The "good news" is that we have been forever forgiven and that believers have the promise of a coming eternal kingdom!

We were not created by God to live a life of separation, sickness, pain and sin. We were not created by God to spend eternity in hell. Jesus fully reveals this truth when He shares with His disciples in John 10:10, "The thief comes only to steal and kill and destroy; I have come that they may have life, and have it to the full." This is why Jesus came to reveal the heart of the Father and reconcile us to Him through His death on the Cross and His Resurrection. The gospel is simple, yet at the same time, we don't want to dilute it.

### There are five easy steps to remember how to share the gospel:

1. We were created for a relationship with God, but sin separated us from our created purpose.
2. Jesus paid the penalty of death in our place at the Cross.
3. We've been forgiven and liberated through His Resurrection and by the power of the Holy Spirit.
4. We're now restored into our created purpose: To love God and love the world around us.
5. Jesus is coming back to restore all things.

When we put our faith in Jesus Christ as the only way to the Father and submit our lives to His leadership, then we can experience forgiveness of sins, the empowerment of the Holy Spirit and live a life of freedom from sin by the influence of His constant grace. When we receive this by faith, we can be baptized and brought into a covenant relationship with our Creator. We can be restored into who we were designed to be when we become a disciple and follower of Jesus.

We will only fully experience heaven on earth when Jesus returns; but the good news is that we don't have to wait, we can experience a glimpse of heaven on earth now because of what Jesus paid for on the cross. When we share this powerful message with others, it can liberate them and launch them into their God-intended destiny. This is a powerful message that is worth sharing!

When I was in the Middle East meeting with global missionaries, one of the leaders taught out of 1 Corinthians 16. The letter closes with the Aramaic word, "*maranatha,*" and the leader pointed out that the word is the most basic explanation of the gospel message. The word can mean two different things, depending on how it is pronounced. One is "The Lord has come" and the other is "The Lord is coming." This is such a clear way to remember how to share the good news. If you don't remember anything else, remember this: The Lord Jesus has come and paid for the sins of the earth. The Lord Jesus is coming again to restore all things. Maranatha! (Come Lord Jesus!)

## Our Gospel Responsibility

> "The Gospel is not good news to people who do not hear it… and an un-preached gospel is no Gospel at all."- Reinhard Bonnke[8]

With this incredible message, we also bear the weight of a great responsibility. This good news is only good for those who actually hear the message. It's only possible for them to hear this message when they have a messenger. God is looking for each of his ambassadors to be bold and to share this message until every nation, tribe and tongue has had a chance to hear.

My prayer for you is that you would grow and taste the joy of sharing this incredibly good news with others!

---

[8] Bonnke, Reinhard. *Evangelism by Fire*. Charisma House, 2011.

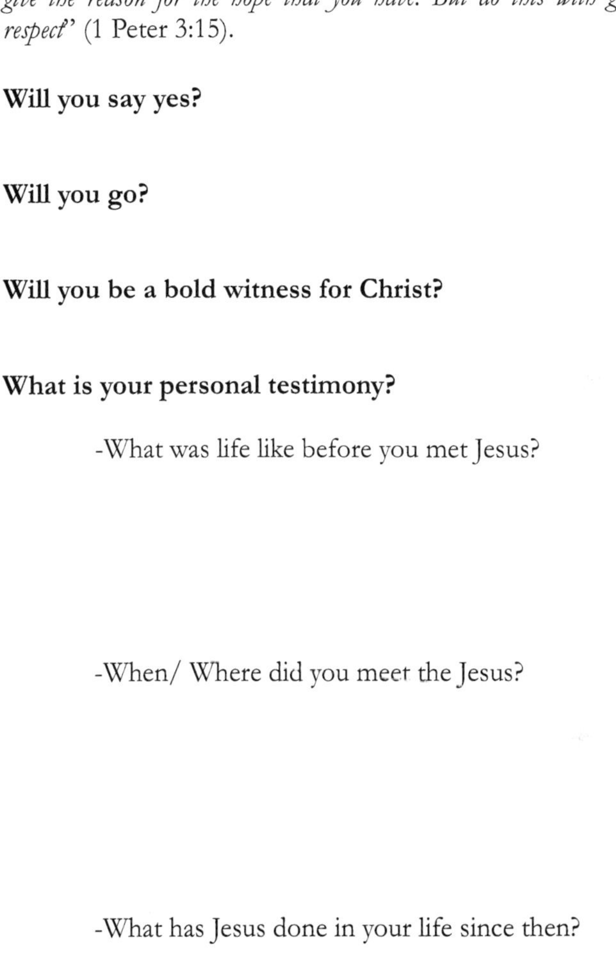

We must "*Always be prepared to give an answer to everyone who asks you to give the reason for the hope that you have. But do this with gentleness and respect*" (1 Peter 3:15).

**Will you say yes?**

**Will you go?**

**Will you be a bold witness for Christ?**

**What is your personal testimony?**

-What was life like before you met Jesus?

-When/ Where did you meet the Jesus?

-What has Jesus done in your life since then?

# 6 - DISCOVERING THE HOLY SPIRIT

In the next few chapters, I want to invite you on my journey of learning how to be led by the Spirit. One of the greatest joys I have experienced has been growing in my relationship with the Holy Spirit. In fact, joy (Gal 5:22-23) is one of the "fruits" of the Holy Spirit and an evidence of Him leading our lives. The more I've been led by Him, the greater the adventures have become and the more joy I have experienced.

The idea of being led by the Spirit of God wasn't something I was familiar with after coming out of my addiction. My perspective of the Holy Spirit was that occasionally, He would tell me when I was doing something wrong, and He would help me understand the Bible. I really limited the work of the Holy Spirit to those two main categories and was not necessarily open to anything more, mainly because I wasn't aware that there *was* more.

I mentioned the story of being baptized in the Holy Spirit in the previous chapter. After that experience one major change that happened immediately was that I began to spend long hours in prayer. No one coached me to do this, and no one around me was doing this either, yet I was overwhelmed with this desire to be with God as much as possible. Before this, I would fall asleep or become distracted even after trying to pray for just a few minutes. The dramatic and instant change in my prayer life was one of the first clear signs of the impact the baptism of the Holy Spirit had on me. Those first few months after this experience, my life was completely transformed as I started to spend hours with God and grow in my relationship with the Holy Spirit.

During this season I wrestled with something that really frustrated and confused me. The more I read the Bible, the more I saw these stories of people experiencing things that were supernatural. The Bible is packed full of miracles, signs, wonders and supernatural occurrences. As I read the Bible stories of the early church and saw all that happened, it begged the question, "Why don't we see the same stuff now if we believe in the same God?" This question plagued me for months. Thankfully, the question drove me deeper and deeper into the Word of God and into prayer.

I honestly had no idea what kind of adventure God was inviting me into with this question, and how much my life would change over the next two years…

## God, is this You?

My first experience with being led by the Holy Spirit was in a time of worship and prayer. We were having weekly gatherings in a home to worship Jesus for extended periods of time. I loved being there and was hungry to know God more. During one particular worship time, a thought came into my mind, "I want you to say something…" At this time, the idea of sharing something in front of even a small group was absolutely terrifying.

I started to question this "voice". I even tried to ignore it. But it kept coming back over and over again. I didn't know exactly what was happening, but I knew for sure I did not want to say anything! Not only that, but I also had no idea what I would say even if I did speak up. I was so caught off guard by this experience, I didn't know how to respond.

Then, in the same way I heard it before, the voice said, "I want you to say something, I'll confirm that it is Me by weeping and tears."

When I heard that, I remember thinking, "What does that even mean?" Suddenly the worship leader in the room stops singing and playing the guitar. The room got awkwardly quiet and he said to us, "I feel like someone needs to share something…" and it clicked, God was speaking to me! I still didn't want to say anything, and had no idea what *to* say, but in that moment I got enough courage to open my mouth. As soon as I started speaking, a surge of power came over my entire body and I found myself saying things I hadn't expected. I spoke with a boldness that was completely unlike me. While I was declaring what God was saying, people all over the room jumped out of their chairs and onto the floor and began to weep.

The sobbing continued all around me as I finished speaking and I remembered then what God had said to me just before the worship leader stopped playing. He wanted me to know that He actually was talking to me and through me to the group. That night I started to realize that God wanted to speak to me in the everyday parts of my life and that He wanted to speak through me to others. This was my first introduction into the joyful reality of representing God by hearing His voice and sharing with others.

## Growing Pains

The idea that God could speak to me in order to give me guidance in everyday situations was life-transforming. Over the next two years, I earnestly launched out on the journey of discovering God's voice more clearly and realizing that the Holy Spirit wanted to be a part of my life every single day. This new season of exploration was filled with joy, incredible testimonies, and also some really humbling experiences. I learned that it was important that I stay open to growing in hearing God's voice while also staying humble and listening to advice and correction.

One weekend I was a leader at a retreat with about 150 teens and young adults. The Holy Spirit was moving so wonderfully in one of the worship times and I noticed a young man in the audience. I felt strongly that I needed to go and share something with him. As I was walking toward him, I sensed that he had a big calling on his life. I shared what I was seeing and then prayed for him and told him I felt like he was going to be a pastor and that God would do big things through Him. He was encouraged and said he appreciated the prayer. I left the event and didn't think about that experience until a few weeks later when I got a phone call.

His pastor called me and wanted to discuss what happened at the retreat and what I had said to that young man. Immediately, I started feeling this need to defend myself and to not listen to what this pastor was saying. He told me that what I said to the young man encouraged him in some ways but also created a lot of anxiety in his life. The pastor asked me to be more careful in the future about telling people what their God-given calling is or what kind of job they would have. As he was sharing with me, I really didn't understand the issue until he started to tell me his own story…

When he was a teenager, a man came to his church and hosted some revival meetings. One night during the revival, he called him out of the crowd and gave him a word that he would be a youth pastor one day. He left that meeting and kept that word in his heart for many years. Later on, this pastor was serving in a very different type of ministry than youth ministry and therefore questioned his ministry assignment because of the word he was given as a teenager. He wondered if maybe he had missed his God-given calling or direction for his life because of this one word he received. He said it took quite some time for him to realize that he actually wasn't supposed to be a youth pastor and to feel confident about what he was doing in life and ministry.

This experience taught me that one of the greatest keys to growing in this area of being led by the Spirit is having people in your life who can give you feedback and counsel. I couldn't agree more with Banning Liebscher, founder of Jesus Culture, when he said, "Receiving feedback and correction is absolutely essential if we want to keep growing."[9]

It's so important that we be established in a local church and in Christian community if we want to grow in the area of hearing God's voice. It's in this environment that we can learn to hear His voice together. It's also in community that we can receive much needed correction and discipline as we're discovering the path of being led by the Holy Spirit.

My encouragement for people that are on the receiving end of a prophetic word from someone else in the Body of Christ is to be open and expectant for God to speak to you. The bible makes it

---

[9] Liebscher, Banning. Rooted: the Hidden Places Where God Develops You. WaterBrook Press, 2016. page 198

clear that the prophetic ministry is for the purpose of encouragement and building up of the Body of Christ. Many times God will want to speak to you and will use those around you to speak to you.

I recommend always filtering any word given to you by asking a few simple questions:

1. Does this word come into alignment with what the word of God teaches?

2. Does this word encourage me and build me up?

3. Does this word confirm other things God has been speaking to me before?

If those three questions are answered with a firm yes, then I would encourage you to write down the word that you have received and begin to pray about this word. Also, take the word you have received to your pastors and spiritual leaders and see what else they may have to say that will encourage you on your journey. Be open and expectant that God wants to speak to you in Christian community!

I realized after hearing this story that I needed to mature in my sensitivity to the Holy Spirit and be more careful about the words I shared with people, not letting my enthusiasm get in the way. I wanted to be used by God and be led by Him in everything! I continued to grow in my journey by boldly taking steps of faith when I sensed Holy Spirit was leading me. Early on, I was often more wrong than I was right. It was such a fun journey discovering the reality that Holy Spirit wanted to lead me and guide me in every area of my life.

## Where are my keys?

One weekend while visiting family in Atlanta, I realized that I could not find my keys. Most of the weekend I didn't worry about it - I just assumed they would show up eventually. I was calm about it until Monday morning came and I had to drive back to work.

I got up that morning, put my things in the car and started searching. I looked under every pillow, every room and every drawer I could find. I couldn't find them anywhere. It got to the point where I started to stress, worried that I wouldn't make it to work on time. I called a locksmith, only to find out that it would be hundreds of dollars for a new key to my car. The more time that passed, the angrier I became.

Finally I went outside feeling defeated. I stood on the front porch and started to talk out loud to God, "God, you know exactly where my keys are. Why haven't you shown me where to find them?" It was a prayer of frustration, and honestly I was almost sarcastic, as if God wasn't going to help me anyway with something as trivial as finding my keys.

Immediately, as soon as I prayed, an image popped into my head. I literally had a flash of an image of my keys under some things I had thrown away when I first arrived at my parents' house in the trash can outside. I had looked in that trash can multiple times, but had not thought to dig all the way down to the bottom.

I decided I might as well look ONE MORE TIME and walked over to the trash can and began pulling things out. I got to the items I had thrown away, picked them up, and guess what was right beneath them? My keys. I was elated *and* blown away! God had answered my sarcastic prayer only moments before. It was shocking to me that God wanted to be a part of even the smaller spaces in my life. He was taking me on a journey of discovering His voice and leading in my everyday life.

## The Voice of the Shepherd

All throughout the scripture, illustrations of shepherds and sheep are used to help paint the picture of God leading His people. It was a very familiar idea to the people of Israel that they quickly related to and understood. When Jesus called His first disciples, they heard Him tell a parable about a good shepherd. When teaching them about the relationship He would have with His followers,He wanted them to understand that HE is the Good Shepherd that would always lead them. They were like His sheep, and they would always be under His care and guidance.

In John 10:3 Jesus states, "*The sheep hear his voice, and he calls his own sheep by name and leads them out. When he has brought out all his own, he goes before them, and the sheep follow him, for they know his voice.*"

This is such a clear picture that Jesus gives us of how our relationship should be with Him every day. We're destined to know the voice of our Shepherd, know what He's saying, and follow Him in everything we do. One of the best ways to get to know His voice is to spend time with Him. The more often you spend time with someone, the more familiar his or her voice will become to you. It works the same way with the voice of God. If we want to grow in our ability to be led by Him, we must start spending more time with Him in the quiet space of prayer. It's in this secret place that we can increasingly discover the voice of the Shepherd.

The moment I surrendered to Christ, I knew that it was His voice I was really responding to. He was the one speaking louder and more clearly than anything or anyone in that moment and I could not resist His calling and His voice. For some reason, I assumed that after that moment, God wouldn't really want to talk to me or lead me. The truth is, that God wanted me to be able to hear and be led by His voice all along.

A few chapters later into the gospel of John, we get a window into the final moments of Jesus' time with His disciples before He was betrayed. During this time, in Chapters 14-16, He kept pointing them to the reality of the promise of the Holy Spirit. He encouraged them with the fact that after His departure, the Father would send them another helper, the Holy Spirit. Jesus reiterated this fact because He knew the Holy Spirit would be the key proponent in the success of the disciples after He left.

We don't have the luxury the disciples had of walking with Jesus here on earth. We don't get to eat with Him, look at Him, ask Him questions and see how He responds in certain situations. So many times when I read the Gospels, I think of how much I would have loved to have been there to see Him and hear Him.

What I've been discovering, however, is that Jesus knew that a life with the Holy Spirit on a daily basis would be far better than actually walking with Him like the disciples did for those three years. He even went so far as to say in John 16:11, "*But very truly I tell you, it is for your good that I am going away. Unless I go away, the Advocate will not come to you; but if I go, I will send him to you.*"

I can just imagine the disciples' puzzlement. How in the world would having the Holy Spirit be better than walking with Jesus in the flesh? I could imagine the tension they felt and how much they desperately did not want Jesus to go anywhere. Jesus was the fulfillment of every longing they had ever had. He was the perfect leader, the perfect friend, the perfect guide. How could it be better if He left?!

The disciples didn't realize the truth of this statement until after Jesus had been crucified, defeated death and ascended to be with the Father. The last thing He told them before He ascended was in Acts 1:4-5, "*Do not leave Jerusalem until the Father sends you the gift he promised, as I told you before. John baptized with water, but in just a few days you will be baptized with the Holy Spirit.*" Jesus wanted them to stay and wait until the promise of the Holy Spirit came upon them. Jesus knew that having the Holy Spirit would be the ultimate game-changer for the early church.

They went to wait together in the upper room for what Jesus had promised - and then suddenly the Holy Spirit came upon them with great power. Immediately they were thrusted into a whole new life of boldness and being led by God in a way they could never have imagined. As you continue reading through the book of Acts, it's clearly evident that the early church lived as closely connected to the Holy Spirit as they did with Jesus himself. They were led by the Holy Spirit daily and they experienced the joy of following His voice.

Phillip, one of the early disciples, is recorded in Acts chapter 8 as having a powerful encounter with a total stranger. He was instructed by the Lord to go to a specific road that went from Jerusalem towards the south. As he obeys the Lord and goes along that road, he encounters a very affluent man from Ethiopia. Phillip notices that the man is reading from the book of Isaiah and "*The Holy Spirit said to Philip, 'Go over and walk along beside the carriage'*" (Acts 8:29). After obeying the Holy Spirit's leading, the man hears the gospel, responds with great joy, and is baptized immediately. The fruit of Phillip's obedience to the leading of the Holy Spirit was that this man was radically born again and was likely responsible for launching one of the oldest Christian churches on the earth in Ethiopia.

What we clearly see the early church doing is a template and model for the way that our lives should look today as Jesus followers. Our hearts should long for our lives to be led by the Holy Spirit in the same way we see the early church being led in scripture. There is a joy that we can access only when we live a life that is led by the Holy Spirit!

## Fisherman Story

This past year I was enjoying a beautiful day off with my family in New England. We were enjoying the warm summer sunshine together in the front yard of my in-laws home outside of Boston. During the afternoon, while we were playing with the kids, a guy we didn't know kept riding his bike over to their property and would leave after a few minutes. He did this several times and I started to wonder what he was doing…

Finally, later in the afternoon, he came back one last time with a fishing pole and we all now understood why he kept coming to look at the pond on their property. He politely waved and asked if we would mind if he fished in the pond. We smiled and told him that it would be fine. We stayed out in the front yard and I was playing with my son Josiah who was around 2 at the time.

Shortly after that, I sensed the Holy Spirit leading me to go over and talk to him while he was fishing from the dock. I can only explain it by saying that I was suddenly filled with a desire to go over and talk to him. I grabbed my little boy's hand and we walked over to watch the fisherman.

When I got over to the dock with my son, we smiled and watched him as he was fishing. Josiah was so excited to see him fishing and was hoping to watch him catch a really big one. I struck up a conversation and noticed he was wearing a wristband that said "1- 800-Recovery." I pointed out the bracelet and he started telling me that he was a member of some recovery meetings. I then shared with him that I had actually been through similar struggles in my past and he started to open up to me about how he had been going through addiction for over ten years. I learned that his name was Ricki.

He told me that he had tried meetings and rehabs, but that he still struggled, going back and forth into his addiction. I began to tell him my story of how I had found a way to total freedom from addiction. He became curious and started to ask questions. I explained to him that Jesus could totally change his life, so much so that he would never have to go back to his addiction again. He told me that he had never thought that was actually possible. I asked him, "Can I share the gospel with you?" He looked at me and said, "Yes…" I said, "Come sit down over here and I'll tell you more…"

Just like that, he put down his pole and sat next to me. I sent my son over to play with his grandfather and I shared the simple gospel with Ricki and asked him, "Do you want to make Jesus the Lord of your life? He's not wanting to just be a part of your life. He wants every part of you. If you put your faith in Him and make Him your Lord, He will change you completely!"

Without hesitation, Ricki responded, "My parents have been Christians since I was in high school, but I just never thought I was ready. But now I realize that I am ready. Yes I want this.. "

I stood up with him next to the pond and we prayed together. He prayed a prayer of faith, declaring his allegiance to Jesus and his desire to be forgiven and made new. At that moment an incredible miracle happened, Ricki was made into a brand new creation, he was born again!

After we prayed, he gave me a big hug, got my phone number, and abruptly jumped on his bike and rode away. I was in total shock. I had no idea or expectation that would happen when the Holy Spirit led me to go over and talk to him.

Back with the family on the front porch, my phone started to ring. I didn't recognize the number, but it was a number from Massachusetts, so I picked it up. I immediately recognized the caller's voice as Ricki's. He said, "Hey man, we're coming over!" I said, "Okay, who's coming over? When?" Suddenly a SUV turns into our driveway and he says, "I went home and told my family what happened and they all wanted to come meet you!"

I smiled as they pulled in. His parents jumped out of the car and started to explain how thankful they were and how they had been praying for years. Our whole family came out and met Ricki's family. There was so much joy!

Ricki introduced me to his brother and said his brother was going through some of the same struggles that he had been going through. He asked me if I would be willing to tell his brother what I had told him. Of course I smiled and led them both over to the front porch. We sat down and I shared the gospel with his brother. I looked at him in the same way I had looked at Ricki and asked him if he also wanted to give his life to Jesus Christ.

His brother accepted Christ right then and there with the same joy. Ricki actually helped me lead his brother to the Lord while we sat there. Afterwards we all experienced a joy that was truly indescribable! There is a joy we can experience when we invite others into the Kingdom of God that is incomparable. Nothing even comes close to the joy of seeing people come out of darkness and into the light of God's love!

Afterward, Ricki said to me, "Andrew I want to be baptized." I smiled and said, "That's awesome bro!" He looked at me seriously and said, "No, I mean like right now." I was kind of shocked, "Okay, like right now? Yes, we can do that! Hold on a minute…"

I ran inside and grabbed some Bibles. I showed him scripture about the new covenant and baptism. I explained to him the purpose of baptism and made sure he understood what it all meant. He told me that he understood and was excited to be baptized.

I took him over to my family and his parents and said, "Ricki wants to get baptized!" His mom smiled and said, "That's great!" I hesitated for a moment and then clarified what I meant, "He wants to get baptized, like, right now…"

She kind of twisted her head and said, "Is that okay?" I laughed and assured her, "Yes! In the scripture most people were baptized the moment after they were born again. I think Ricki is ready." I could tell this was a new concept for her, but she laughed and agreed.

We grabbed a towel from the house and led Ricki over to the pond, the *very spot we met just an hour before.* His family and my family all gathered on the bank of the pond. Ricki and I jumped into the pond, and within seconds, we were both up to our ankles in slimy pond mud. We waded over to the spot where he had been fishing and I prayed with him and shared with both families all that God had just done. The moment was surreal. The Holy Spirit had led me to go talk to him as he was fishing and now he's being baptized and his whole family is there to witness it!

We baptized him in the pond and both households were overjoyed! God did a miracle in Ricki's life that day and it all started with a simple response to the leading of the Holy Spirit. God wants to invite us into a life where we are following His leading in the everyday moments of our lives. He wants to use our lives to see the supernatural reality of His kingdom displayed everywhere we go. He's just waiting for us to become more open to the leading of His Spirit.

## Don't Overthink or Over Spiritualize it...

Along this journey of learning to be led by the Holy Spirit, one of my greatest temptations has been to over complicate everything. For me, this can be one of the first things that will actually stifle my ability to hear God's voice and to be led by Him. I once heard missionary Heidi Baker share that those who want to learn to hear God's voice and be led by Him must stay childlike in their relationship to God. She makes the analogy of how people who are trying to learn new languages must remain childlike and be willing to step out and take risks with their new language.

When people are unwilling to be childlike and instead remain reserved, they will take far longer in mastering a new language than those who are willing to be childlike in their discovery and learning. God wants us to be willing to take risks and to even be wrong. He wants us to be willing to learn and grow in hearing His voice in a childlike manner.

*"For all who are led by the Spirit of God are sons of God. For you did not receive the spirit of slavery to fall back into fear, but you have received the Spirit of adoption as sons, by whom we cry, 'Abba! Father!' The Spirit himself bears witness with our spirit that we are children of God, and if children, then heirs--heirs of God and fellow heirs with Christ, provided we suffer with him in order that we may also be glorified with him" (Romans 8:14-17.*

We can clearly see the connection in Romans 8 between being led by the Holy Spirit and being childlike. Our ability to hear God and respond to His voice in obedience is directly connected to our childlike faith. When we live our lives in this way, we can experience His voice daily and discover the joy of being led by Him.

Because we are His children, He will lead us. His leading is proof that we are His. The scripture makes it clear that if we are His, then we should have a life that is being led by His Spirit. For us to not be led by the Spirit and yet say we are His children is unbiblical. The Holy Spirit is the proof in our lives that we are born again and are God's children. It's hard to imagine that we could have the Holy Spirit in our lives and not be influenced and led by Him.

The most direct way that the Holy Spirit speaks to us and leads us on a daily basis is through scripture. The Holy Spirit used many authors over thousands of years to transcribe the very Word of God and He uses these inspired words to lead us and guide us still today. Psalm 119:105 says, "*Your word is a lamp to my feet and a light to my path.*" The Word of God is our ultimate guide in life and is the foundation for everything else that we sense God leading us to do. If we sense "God" is "leading" us to do something that doesn't line up with the clear themes and guidelines of scripture, then it must not be God leading us. For example, if someone senses God is leading them to steal from someone or to cheat on their spouse, because that comes against the Word of God, it cannot be the Holy Spirit leading that person.

When it comes to being led by the Spirit, scripture helps us in so many ways. There are very clear instructions that make waiting for a voice from heaven, an angel, or an image in our minds unnecessary. Jesus made it clear that we are to make disciples, be witnesses, serve the poor, love our enemies and forgive those who hurt us. We don't need any further "leading" or "prompting" in order to follow these instructions.

An example that Jesus gave us is the story He told about the Good Samaritan. This is a parable that teaches us the principle that if we see someone in need, we shouldn't pass them by, but should offer to help them. Jesus teaches us through this passage that obeying the commandment to love our neighbor should actually look like something tangible. Again, Heidi Baker says, "Love looks like something." We don't need any further instructions than just reading scripture to know we should stop to help those in need, to take care of the widows and orphans, and to love those who hate us. We don't need a voice from heaven to instruct us to make disciples and share the gospel with those around us. Those types of things are clear instructions from Jesus found in the gospels and we are to obey on a daily basis.

In addition to being led by the voice of the Spirit through scripture, we also get to go on fun adventures with God as He leads and guides us daily in new ways. It's not just one or the other. It's both. We are to live a life of simple obedience to what is clear in scripture and also be open to the leading of the Holy Spirit.

When we see the story of the Holy Spirit leading Paul in Acts 16, we also discover that sometimes He tells us no. We may desire to do certain things or go in certain directions but at times He will instruct us not to. I am so grateful for the many occasions in my life where the Holy Spirit has led me by giving me a clear "no" to an open door or idea that I had. When I reflect back, I'm so grateful for the times where I obeyed Him even when he asked me not to move in certain directions. I now can see that He always knows what is best for me.

The last thing I want to say about this specific subject is that we shouldn't ever become so "spiritual" or "spirit-led" that we cannot serve in practical ways and walk in obedience to those in leadership over us. For years, I've seen people discover the amazing reality of being spirit-led, yet not be able to hold a job or to do simple tasks to serve their local church. I've also seen people make commitments to others and then at the very last minute back out of those commitments and say the "Holy Spirit" led them to do something else. These types of behavior are not the fruit of a life of being spirit led, but rather signs of immaturity. God is raising up children of God who are led by the Spirit and have a heart to serve in the most simple of ways. May we never become so "spiritual" that we begin to neglect the basic things we need to take care of in life. God wants us to walk in wisdom and with a heart full of humility as we discover the joy of being led by Him!

## Some practical ways to grow with the Holy Spirit:

1. Spend time with the Lord. Nothing will help you grow more in hearing God's voice and being led by Him than simply being with Him. Begin to give yourself more time each day to pray, read the Bible and worship. It's in these times that you will grow in your ability to hear His voice.

2. Practice hearing God's voice in the small things. Start asking Him daily for His advice, His wisdom, His leading in the most simple things. Ask Him to help you make a simple decision and then *wait* for Him to lead you. When you miss it or you blow it, remember that nothing can separate you from the love of God. Be willing to humbly admit you missed it, be reassured of God's love, and be willing to step out again.

3. Take risks. Look for chances to step outside of your comfort zone. Let Him lead you more in your everyday life while you are shopping or just out walking in your neighborhood. Invite God into these everyday simple moments and start to step out when He leads you to say something to someone or to pray for them.

# 7 - DISCOVERING THE PROPHETIC

In this chapter, I want to share some key things I've learned on this journey of discovering the prophetic gift that is given by the Holy Spirit. Earlier, I mentioned a story about God speaking to me in the midst of a time of worship with some friends. For me that was one of the first experiences where God spoke to me and through me to others. It was the first time I was used by God in the gift of prophecy. At the time that it happened, I had no idea what the gift of prophecy really was, or even the purpose of the gift. Let's go on a journey in discovering more about this incredible gift that is given by the Holy Spirit…

The simplest way to explain the prophetic is this: we listen to God, hear what God has to say, and then share with others what we heard from Him. *Listen, hear, say.* God desires for every person to know Him and encounter Him. Many times, God uses people as His messengers to reach others. We see this all throughout the scripture. Jonah was sent to Nineveh as God's messenger. John the Baptist was sent to announce the arrival of Jesus the Messiah to the people of Israel. Sharing prophetic words in the New Testament was an instrumental part of the early church movement.

In the book of Acts, something extraordinary was recorded during the birth of the early church. They were all waiting in a room together praying for weeks after Jesus' ascension. After a time, we're told that suddenly the Holy Spirit came upon each of them "like a mighty rushing wind." People from all over the city heard them shouting and praising God in their native languages and were confused by what was going on. Peter stands up and boldly declares that what they were experiencing was the fulfillment of what Joel had prophesied:

*"And it shall come to pass afterward, that I will pour out my Spirit on all flesh; your sons and your daughters shall prophesy, your old men shall dream dreams, and your young men shall see visions. Even on the male and female servants in those days I will pour out my Spirit" (Joel 2:28-29).*

Everything changed when the early church began to experience the outpouring of the Holy Spirit. When God poured out the Holy Spirit upon the church, He opened up the ability for everyday people, sons and daughters, male and female, to prophesy. In generations past, only a very select few could prophesy. Now, because of the outpouring of the Holy Spirit, those who received the Holy Spirit would be able to do so. This is such an amazing thing that God did for the early church! The exciting reality is that the Holy Spirit also wants to empower today's church! He wants to empower *you* to prophesy, see visions, and dream things inspired by God.

## Starting to step out

Several years ago when I really started to "eagerly desire the gifts" (1 Cor 14:1) and became open to God using me, some incredible things started to happen. One night after our prayer meeting, I was in a pizza place with some friends . We sat and enjoyed eating pizza and catching up together. After paying for our bill, we started to make our way out of the restaurant, but before I left, I noticed two girls in their mid- twenties as they were sitting down at their table. I instantly had this sense that I needed to go and talk to them.

I had no idea what to say to these girls, but the longer I hesitated, the more I just "knew" in my heart that I needed to go talk to them. Suddenly a thought popped into my head as I took notice of one of the girls: "Her boyfriend just broke up with her and I want you to tell her that I love her and see her." I was kind of in shock by the thought that came into my head and was now really curious as to whether or not this was from the Lord.

I nervously walked toward them, thinking, "Well Andrew, this could either go really good or really bad…" When I got over to their table they both stopped and looked at me. I just smiled awkwardly and said, "So sorry to bother you…" As I spoke, they were friendly and were waiting to hear what I had to say. I didn't want them to get the wrong Idea, like I was approaching them to get their number or something, so I said, "I'm not trying to hit on you guys, I just honestly felt like God wanted me to come over and share something with you."

Looking toward the girl, I said, "I feel like God showed me that you just went through a breakup in a relationship and He wants me to tell you that He sees you and that He loves you so much. "

Her friend responded, "Oh my God!" and lifted her hand to cover her mouth. She looked at her friend and then back at me. I didn't know what to say, so I just waited to let her speak. "We were just outside before we came in to eat and she (her friend) was on the phone with her boyfriend. They broke up right before we came in. This was just like a minute ago."

The girl started to cry, so I reiterated what God had said to share with her. It was obvious that this was a moment where God really wanted her to encounter His love and to know that He sees her. After talking another minute or two, I thanked them for letting me interrupt their meal together and prayed for the girl. Even more surprised than the girls, I walked away with a joy that stirred up in me a deep and profound hunger to see God use me more in that way.

## The Power of Words to Create

*"Then God said, 'Let us make man in our image, after our likeness. And let them have dominion over the fish of the sea and over the birds of the heavens and over the livestock and over all the earth and over every creeping thing that creeps on the earth'" So God created man in his own image, in the image of God he created him; male and female he created them. And God blessed them. And God said to them, 'Be fruitful and multiply and fill the earth and subdue it, and have dominion over the fish of the sea and over the birds of the heavens and over every living thing that moves on the earth'" (Genesis 1:26-28).*

When God created the galaxies and stars, He used his spoken word and they came to exist. When God created the heavens and the earth, they were created because He declared it and they were made. He didn't have to create things with His words but chose to do it in this way. God could have made everything just with a simple thought. He chose instead to declare things into existence and to demonstrate the power of the spoken word to create substance and life.

After creating the skies, the earth, the oceans, land and living creatures, He created mankind– the only creation that God made in His "image" or "likeness." When He created man, He had something special in mind. He formed man out of dust and breathed His life into them. From the beginning of the scripture, it is clear that God intended for mankind to bear the very image of Himself and to reflect who He is on the earth.

Over and over again, we read in the first chapter of the Bible, "And God said…" When God wanted to create, He simply declared and it came to pass. This phrase is directly connected to the creative nature of who God is and demonstrates the very way that God has decided His creativity should be expressed.

One of the profound realities we see throughout the scripture is that not only is God's Word powerful, but He has also placed a measure of power within the words of mankind. It's as if when He created us in His image and likeness, He also distributed a small measure of His own power for us to create with His words. One of the most famous of all the proverbs is, "*Death and life are in the power of the tongue, and those who love it will eat its fruits*" (Proverbs 18:21). What we speak has the power to create things, both good and bad. We're reminded throughout scripture to watch what we say and to be sure that we're using our speech to declare and bring about good things.

God has given us our words to declare and bring about life, healing, and restoration. They can also bring destruction. It says in Proverbs 12:18-19, "*There is one whose rash words are like sword thrusts, but the tongue of the wise brings healing. Truthful lips endure forever, but a lying tongue is but for a moment.*" Our words are meant to bring health and healing to all those around us. God wants to invite each of us to partner with Him to create life and sustenance through the words that we share each day.

One of my favorite all time stories from the Bible is found in 2 Chronicles 20. This famous story about King Jehoshaphat of Judah records a time when they were totally surrounded by their enemies and seemingly had no hope of survival. In response, the king declares a nationwide time of prayer and fasting. During that time of fasting, the Holy Spirit falls on one man in their midst and empowers him to prophesy to the king and to the entire nation. That man's name was Jahaziel.

When the Holy Spirit came upon Jahaziel, he began to prophesy and declare the Word of God. After he finishes his declaration, the whole nation erupts in worshipful response to what he declared. This short prophetic word gave them the courage and boldness they needed to obey the Lord and confront their enemies. One of the most powerful purposes for our words is to help inspire and create courage in the hearts of others to follow God's plans for their lives. God wants to use each and every person who has the Holy Spirit to speak, declare, and release creativity and boldness over others.

To illustrate this point even further, when I was preparing my whole family for a mission trip throughout east and central Africa, we needed to get the kids an extensive amount of preventative medication and supplies for the journey. While waiting with the kids in the long line at the pharmacy, rather than getting frustrated, I started praying for and ministering to those who were sitting around me. People were so thankful for the prayers and I got to encourage a few by sharing some prophetic words with them. When we were finally checking out, I knew I wanted to encourage the woman at the register. I'm sure that most people act generally annoyed with her because of the long lines and the fact they are not feeling well. I wanted her to really encounter God's love and goodness so I just started to share with her and then prayed with her before we left.

More than a year later, I got an unexpected email from her that illustrates the power of our spoken words and the lasting impact it can have on someone. here's the email:

*My name is M.T., you may not remember me. I met you and your beautiful family one afternoon when I was a pharmacy technician at Walgreens on Wynnton Rd in Columbus as you guys were getting ready for a trip out of the country. You prayed for me and gave some amazing, life-changing advice including your card before you left. I wanted to say "THANK YOU!" I had been fighting the calling on my life before we met. But, after you left it confirmed what He was telling me. It has helped me daily in this current season of my life when my job was taken away due to an injury while trying to raise three boys, pay for college tuition, bills, etc. I've procrastinated and missed precious moments in my children's lives because of work, fear of lack, rejection and doubt that I wasn't good enough. My mistake was looking at my job as the source when it was only a resource. The Source is my Heavenly Father. I'm still battling myself with the calling - I don't want to disappoint Him. I won't keep you any longer. Thank you again for your kindness and thoughtfulness.*

*Sincerely,*
*M.T.*

## Purpose of the Prophetic

As we begin to journey into understanding more and more about the gift of prophecy, it's important that we understand the purpose. Each gift that God gives us through the Holy Spirit comes with it's own intended purpose. Several places in the scripture help us to understand more about the gifts and their purposes.

One of the most clear passages that help us to understand the gifts of the Holy Spirit, including prophecy, is found in 1 Corinthians 12-14. (I'd encourage you to stop and actually take a moment to read the entire three chapters together.)

*Pursue love, and earnestly desire the spiritual gifts, especially that you may prophesy. For one who speaks in a tongue speaks not to men but to God; for no one understands him, but he utters mysteries in the Spirit. On the other hand, the one who prophesies speaks to people for their upbuilding and encouragement and consolation. (1Co 14:1-3 ESV)*

Imagine getting lost in the woods while on a hiking adventure and having a compass in your backpack, but not knowing what it's for. Without understanding the intended purpose of that compass, you likely would never even look to utilize it to help you navigate back to where you need to be. Once you understand the intended purpose of the compass, then you can start to learn to use it to find your way.

Understanding God's intended purpose for the gift of prophecy inspires us to desire and grow in using the gift. The primary purpose of prophecy is to encourage and build others up *in love*. You'll be relieved to know that it's not about us! Prophecy is a gift that is not for us, but is given to us for others. In 1 Corinthians 14:4, it says that the gift of tongues is for our own building up but that prophecy is intended to build up others. In other words, the gift is not given to us for our own benefit, but so that we can use it to bless others.

*The gift of prophecy can help provide anchors of hope in people's faith journey that will help them stay the course.* Many times people sense a calling of God in their lives or that they need to go in a certain direction, but then face a lot of adversity when they begin moving in that direction. A prophetic word can help them stay the course and encourage them along the way. Never underestimate the power of how God wants to use you in this gift and never apologize for seeking to grow in this gift.

The Apostle Paul clearly tells the church in 1 Corinthians 14:1,39 to earnestly desire to be used by the Holy Spirit through the gift of prophecy. This is by far one of the most clear encouragements that the Apostle Paul made to the church. I believe that he expressed this in his letter because he knew how hard things would become and how much the church would need the edification and encouragement that the gift of prophecy can bring.

The purpose of prophecy is also so that unbelievers will be drawn to give their lives to God. Paul exhorts the church that if an unbeliever experiences the gift of prophecy, "...he is convicted by all, he is called to account by all, the secrets of his heart are disclosed, and so, falling on his face, he will worship God and declare that God is really among you" (1 Corinthians 14:23-25 version). God can use us in powerful ways to encourage others and draw people to Himself when we begin to step out and use this gift.

As a recap, there are three purposes of prophecy laid out in 1 Corinthians 14:

1. To encourage, edify and build others up in their faith.

2. To help others. It's not a gift that is directly beneficial for us.

3. To draw unbelievers to Christ and to demonstrate how real God is.

## Three Steps to Growing in Prophecy

When I first began to explore the gifts of the Holy Spirit, I thought that each of the gifts were out of my reach or beyond my ability to grasp. I thought that maybe the gifts were somehow only for the "super" Jesus followers and pastors, but couldn't be for an everyday person like myself. What's been so joyful is that I've discovered more and more just how simple it all really is.

There are three simple steps that have really helped me to grow in this gift and discover more of the prophetic.

**The first step: Make time for taking risks.** I want to encourage you to be willing to take risks. We can only grow in the gift of prophecy when we start to put ourselves in situations where we can be used. Allow time in each day to let God start to draw you to people that you work with or total strangers in public settings. Begin to look for those places where God is already working and where He wants to invite you in to partner with Him. When He starts to lead you to someone or seems to "highlight" a person to you, begin to follow His leading by going over to them and striking up a conversation. Many times, God will even lead you to someone before giving you a prophetic word just to see if you are willing to take the risk and go over to talk to them.

**The second step: Listen to what you sense God is saying to you for someone else.** For a long time I was really overwhelmed by the simple idea of listening to God. I thought it was some sort of mystical thing that only super-Christians could do. What I've discovered is that God is very often speaking, but I am often not listening. Many times I can be so busy with my own thoughts, plans, and schedule.

When we begin to listen to the Lord, He may sometimes speak to us through an impression, a vision, an idea, a memory, a feeling, a thought, a scripture, or many other ways. Begin to become more open to listening to God in your everyday life and watch how His subtle whispers can help you discover the joy of the prophetic.

**The third step: Start to share what you hear from the Lord.** To grow in the gift of prophecy you will need to start sharing what you sense God is saying to you.

It seems so simple, but also can be the most challenging for those of us who don't like to step outside of our comfort zone. In order for us to grow in the gift, we must start to both use and exercise it. When we begin to declare prophetic words with humility *and* remain teachable, we can start to really discover and grow in the prophetic.

## Fort Lauderdale Beach Encounter

After traveling to Haiti with a mission team, we had an extended layover in Fort Lauderdale beach on our return trip. We had spent our time in Haiti traveling, sharing the gospel and working at a Help4Haiti inc. orphanage that was being built. I remember experiencing intense culture shock in Florida after being in Haiti for a week. Within a few hours we went from one of the poorest nations on earth to one of the wealthiest cities. It was hard to adjust as we walked around, noticing for the first time the luxury that we had taken for granted in our nation.

I started to feel a bit frustrated about being back in America. It was hard for me to re-adjust, feeling overwhelmed by the reality that we live in such wealth while people in Haiti, and all over the world, are just struggling to survive. For a few minutes I even started to feel a bit resentful towards my own nation and my own people. After walking around for a while with a bad attitude, I realized I needed to ask the Lord for a new perspective.

As we stood on a street corner getting ready to cross the intersection, I began to quietly pray and sensed an urgency to just go and minister to someone. It was as if the Lord wanted me to change my focus to loving those who were around me right then. I looked across the intersection and noticed a woman sitting down on a concrete ledge and felt the need to go talk to her. I grabbed my friend Caleb and we headed toward the woman.

As I approached her, I had no idea what to say. I vaguely knew that God was leading me to her, but now as I took each step I became painfully aware that I was stepping way outside of my comfort zone and taking a risk. I asked the Lord what He wanted me to say, but absolutely nothing came to mind. When we got to her I still had no idea what to say.

I smiled and said, "Hello…" She looked up at me and suddenly her face became angry and annoyed. She said something like, "What do you want!?" As soon as Caleb saw her expression, he started pretending he didn't know me and walked away. (Looking back, I can't help but laugh at the situation, but in the moment I felt totally left in the deep end!) I still didn't really know what to say, but then the Lord gave me a word about a relationship issue that she was facing and how He wanted to be first in her life. She started to cry uncontrollably. It was at that moment I knew the Holy Spirit was up to something.

The longer I spoke, the more it seemed that the Holy Spirit took control of the situation. It was as if He was just waiting for me to step out and take a risk before He would begin to really speak through me. After about a minute, Caleb came back over to us and looked incredulously at her, then me and said,. "What happened?" The woman described how what I had spoken to her about her relationship had literally just happened only moments before and that she knew it was the Lord speaking to her. We were both blown away.

Afterward, I sensed that God gave me a word of knowledge that she was a singer and used to sing in the church, but had quit singing some time before. She told me that it was true and I started to prophesy that God wanted her to use her gift of singing again. At the end, she eagerly let us pray for her, thanked us for stopping, apologized for her original reaction, and told us that just moments before we met her she had been in a huge fight with her boyfriend. It's encounters like these that continue to stir a deep hunger in me to discover more about the gift of prophecy!

## Dreams, Visions, Dream Interpretation and the Prophetic

*"I will pour out my Spirit on all flesh; your sons and your daughters shall prophesy, your old men shall dream dreams, and your young men shall see visions" (Joel 2).*

The Spirit of God empowered Daniel to interpret dreams even though he was embedded in the midst of the wickedness of Babylon. Joseph was able to have dreams as a boy and was able to interpret them while imprisoned in Egypt. The early disciples of Jesus were instructed and led by dreams and visions while on their missionary journeys. All throughout the scripture, we see that when the Holy Spirit comes upon someone, supernatural things start to take place. They begin to prophesy, they have visions, they dream dreams and are able to interpret them. I believe that every person who has entered into a covenant relationship with Jesus and has received the power of the Holy Spirit, can begin to be used in this way.

As I was preparing to go on my first mission trip to Africa, I had my first prophetic dream. I needed to raise thousands of dollars and was overwhelmed, not knowing how I could possibly raise the money. In the dream, I was speaking at my parents' large home church in Atlanta and realized I wasn't afraid. Up to that point, one of my greatest fears in life was public speaking. Later, sensing that I should call the pastor, I asked him if I could come share about my trip, and although he initially said no, by the end of our conversation he invited me to come speak. In spite of being absolutely terrified in the weeks leading up to it, when I stood on the platform, it was just as it had been in the dream! Interestingly, over the past few years I've had many dreams that have shown me what was to come and given me direction.

In addition to our own, God can also help us to interpret others' dreams, often revealing their prophetic destiny. One of the most powerful stories in the book of Daniel is when he and all the other interpreters were given the assignment to interpret a dream without actually being told what the dream was. Miraculously, Daniel was shown the dream and given an interpretation. I believe that this same kind of reality is available to Christians today through the working of the Holy Spirit in our lives.

One day while I was working in the downtown area where I lived, I had several meetings throughout the day with various people at the same coffee shop. Each time I walked to or from the coffee shop I would see a certain young woman, and each time I noticed her, I sensed God wanted me to go and talk to her. All day I tried to ignore the reality of the Holy Spirit's persistence in trying to get me to go talk to her!

Reluctantly, and without knowing what I was supposed to say to her, I finally told the Lord in my heart, "I'll go talk to her if I see her one more time." As I'm walking back to my office with the friend I had been meeting with, he started talking about a dream he recently had. As soon as he said the word "dream," I felt the Lord say, "She has been having a recurring dream and I want you to go and talk to her about it." My heart raced and I started thinking about what I was going to say to her while my friend kept talking.

Sure enough, I spotted her and we walked over toward the marketplace booths where she was. I felt so unsure about the word I had heard from the Lord about her. Pausing at another booth, I looked over and noticed some odd things on her table and realized her table was filled with candles and items used for witchcraft. When I saw that I honestly wanted to walk the other way. I finally got the courage to walk up to her table and said, "Hello, I felt like God wanted me to come over and talk to you. I know this may seem really weird but I felt like He told me you have been having a recurring dream…"

As soon as I started talking about the recurring dream, I could tell that I had her attention. Then the craziest thing happened. As I was talking, what looked like movie images started to flash through my mind. I described them to her as if it were her recurring dream. I told her about the house that I saw and various other parts of the dream, describing how the dream felt and how dark it was. When I finished, all the pictures disappeared from my mind and asked her, "Does any of that make sense to you?"

She looked at me, almost angry, and said, "Yes."

"Is this the dream you keep having?"

She paused and said, "Yes."

Inside I was completely blown away, but tried to keep my composure. I kind of wanted to shout as I started to realize what God was doing, but just asked her a simple question, "Do you feel like you need to forgive someone?"

"Yes."

I led her into a prayer of forgiveness and told her, "I really feel like God is trying to use this moment to get your attention and show you that His power is far greater than anything else you are looking toward."

I continued talking to her for a few minutes and found out she was raised at a large local church. I took time to explain to her that God was calling her out of darkness and into His light, and let her know, in a very direct way, that she needed to turn from all witchcraft and repent. I also told her that God loved her and wanted what was best for her. Many of the things I was saying to her were very intense, but because of what had just supernaturally happened, I knew that I had her full attention and permission to speak into her life. She wasn't ready to surrender to Jesus, but I know that moment was a key marker God will use in her life to continue to call her back into His loving arms.

What I've discovered through some of these encounters is that many times God will use supernatural occurrences in the prophetic to really get someone's attention. In five seconds of supernatural activity, God can short-cut what might otherwise take years of relational building. Normally, I would never be so direct with a girl who is a complete stranger, but after seeing what happened and how powerfully God wanted to get her attention, I had this increased boldness to speak very directly and call her to repent.

When the Holy Spirit begins to work through our lives prophetically, we begin to see things happen in a matter of moments that otherwise may have taken years to accomplish. Prophecy, dreams, visions, and words of knowledge invite the supernatural reality of heaven into situations. That's why, I believe, the scripture is so clear in telling us that we are to earnestly desire to be used in this gift.

## Avoiding disillusionment and discouragement

Over the years I have had some pretty incredible encounters where I have seen God use myself and others in the prophetic. I have also had many instances where I got a word wrong or mis-said something. I've had to overcome times of feeling discouraged or as if God didn't want to use me in this way.

One thing I've learned to do when ministering to someone and giving them a prophetic word is to always preface anything I share by saying, "I sense God wanting me to share with you something, but I want to acknowledge that I'm not totally sure." Then after I share something with them I always ask to see if this confirms something in their lives or really speaks to them. I always want to be careful that I'm never leading someone astray or sharing with someone something that could be a distraction. Humility and discernment are paramount.

I could tell countless stories of times where I sensed God leading me to go to someone and share something with someone that ended up being a total blunder. I many times then take those situations back to the Lord in prayer and talk to others about my experiences. I never want discouragement and a lack of faith to cause me to become resistant to the working of the Holy Spirit in my life. It's vital and important that we remain teachable, humble and also driven by a hope-filled perspective.

### Three ways to grow in Dreams, Visions and Prophetic encounters:

In conclusion for this chapter on the prophetic, I want to offer a few simple tips that I believe will help you grow in this area. I want to encourage you to do the following:

1. PRAY --- Ask the Lord for dreams, visions and to be used in the prophetic gift! Begin to pray for God to give you more direction through dreams, visions and encounters. I ask the Lord daily for these and it's been amazing how much they have increased since I started asking for them.

2. GATHER --- Find others who are having dreams from the Lord and start connecting with them. There's something powerful that happens when we get into a community of people who are open to the gifts of the Holy Spirit and His leading in their lives through dreams and visions.

3. RISK --- Start stepping out when God leads you to prophetically share with others. Take risks in dream interpretation and even be open to God showing you what someone else has dreamed before they even tell you!

## Activity:

1- Take 3-5 Minutes to stop and pray for a close friend or family member. As you pray ask God if there is a scripture, a picture or a word He wants you to share with them. Don't overthink this and simply write down what you sense, hear or see with your imagination. Then take a RISK and send them this message with a text or however you feel led. Do this before you move on to the next chapter. Right down what happens below:

2- Go shopping today or to a public space. Ask God to highlight a specific person for you and then ask Him to give you a word for that person. Write down any notes or scriptures. Take the RISK and go share it with them. Do this before you move on to the next chapter. Right down what happens below:

# 8 - DISCOVERING HEALING

My journey in discovering God's power to bring about physical and emotional healing began during a season of focused prayer and studying the Bible. I had been committed to following Jesus for about a year and my hunger to know Him was increasing more and more each day. I knew that I was only scratching the surface of who He is. It was a beautiful season where the Lord was really calling me closer to Himself and teaching me some foundational things that have proved to be essential for everything that I'm doing today.

One of the gnawing questions that started to affect me during that season was, "God, I'm reading about all of these people getting radically healed and set free in scripture but I haven't seen it happen in real life. If the Bible is true and if You are real, then the same things that we see in scripture should still be happening today." It was from this sense of dissatisfaction with the status quo that I began discovering the power of God in a greater measure than I ever could have anticipated.

Not too long after starting to ask these questions, I witnessed my very first miracle. I was living in an environment where miracles were not exactly expected. I'd yet to even witness people praying for the sick. Yet it was as if the Holy Spirit was leading me along a path to discover the supernatural reality of God, in spite of my surroundings and circumstances.

My roommate at the time had to have some emergency dental work done and when he got home, instead of his pain diminishing each day, it only got worse. Eventually, his pain was agonizing and could barely do anything. When he called his dentist, he was told that his mouth had not properly healed from the procedure and to come into the office so he could fix the issue. But God…

Before he left, I felt the urge to pray for him. I laid hands on him and asked God for a miracle. I had been studying the Word of God and had read accounts of miracles happening through the name of Jesus over and over again. Why not here? Why not now?

I asked him if I could pray and he was grateful for the offer. I put my hands on his cheekbone where the pain was and started to pray. I didn't really know *what* to pray for, and I don't remember what I said, but it was short and simple. I had never had this modeled for me so I just made something up on the spot, hoping it would work! When I was done, he told me he appreciated the prayer.

A few minutes later he told me that it actually felt better. At first, I was in shock and then I kind of doubted him. I told him he could tell me the truth and he didn't have to say that to make me feel good about my prayer. He reassured me that it actually did feel better. Later I found out he canceled his dentist appointment and was completely pain-free from the moment we prayed together. He never did have to go to the dentist for that issue. I was more surprised than anyone else by what God did!

## Following the Way of Jesus

In the Gospel of John, starting in chapter 11, Jesus begins entering into the final stage of his three years of public ministry. When Jesus resurrected his friend Lazarus in the city of Bethany, just outside of Jerusalem, the religious leaders began to plan and scheme how they could get rid of this rabbi from Nazareth who so many were beginning to follow. For the religious leaders, they saw Jesus as a threat to their way of life and everything they stood for. Jesus didn't teach as so many of the religious leaders of His day did, rather he taught with true authority and power. He didn't just use words to articulate His message but He also confirmed it through demonstrations of power and miracles.

It was during these last few days that Jesus washes His disciples' feet and their personal paradigms were flipped upside down. The opposite of everything they had seen exemplified in their current religious system, their own teacher and leader insisted on washing their feet. Every leader they saw used their power and influence for their own gain and demanded that others be subservient to them. Jesus showed them a better way and insisted that if they were really going to be His followers that they must follow His example.

After washing their feet, He describes to them that He would be betrayed and denied, and then enters into one of His final teachings. Jesus clearly shares with His disciples who He really is and then one of the most powerful statements in all of scripture:

*"Truly, truly, I say to you, whoever believes in me will also do the works that I do; and greater works than these will he do, because I am going to the Father. Whatever you ask in my name, this I will do, that the Father may be glorified in the Son. If you ask me anything in my name, I will do it" (John 14:12-14 ).*

There are a lot of incredible statements and amazing promises Jesus made throughout scripture. For me, this one statement, made just before the cross, is one of the greatest promises. Jesus wanted his followers to know that He was living His life in a certain way, not for them to just marvel at, but that they would begin to imitate His teachings, generosity, miracles, signs, and wonders everywhere they went.

The "works" that Jesus describes in this passage is pointing directly to the things He did during His three years of ministry. He wanted His disciples to know that they would go and do the same works, and even greater works, than what He had done. Talk about an empowering and servant-hearted leader!

When we look at the life of Jesus, then we can better understand what He was talking about in these final moments with His followers. Most of what we see in the life of Jesus concerning "works" that He did were directly connected to miracles, signs, and wonders. The supernatural works that Jesus did so far outweigh "natural" deeds He performed that it makes no sense to claim that what Jesus was describing to His followers was simply nice things they could do for others.

Peter, one of Jesus' closest friends, later helped to summarize this whole point when he was describing the life of Jesus to a man and his family in the tenth chapter of Acts. He told them, "God anointed Jesus of Nazareth with the Holy Spirit and with power. He went about doing good and healing all who were oppressed by the devil, for God was with him. And we are witnesses of all that he did both in the country of the jews and in Jerusalem" (Acts 10:38-39).

Jesus did miracles and encouraged His disciples to do the same for one simple reason—to glorify the Father. He tells His disciples in John 14:13-14, "Whatever you ask in my name, this I will do, that the Father may be glorified in the son. If you ask me anything in my name, I will do it." Jesus wanted his disciples to be very clear on their purpose. It was not for their own glory or fame; it wasn't for money or a great following. It was not so they could appear to be more godly or holy. It was for one purpose—to glorify the Father of all creation in the name of His only Son, Jesus Christ.

We can also look at a very short testimony in John 9 of a lot of powerful things Jesus did. The disciples were walking with Jesus and noticed a blind man. They ask Him if it was because of his own sin or maybe his parents' mistakes that the man was blind. Jesus responds to them by saying, "It was not that this man sinned, or his parents, but that the works of God might be displayed in him. We must work the works of him who sent me…" (John 9:3-4).

There are two things we can learn from this statement. First, we are reminded that the purpose of a miracle is to display the works of God and to bring Him glory. Secondly, we see here that Jesus directly connected the word "works" to the performing of miracles, signs, and wonders. This passage helps us understand that Jesus performed all of His miracles in His ministry to bring glory to the Father and to set an example for us in the way that we would live our lives, if we believe in Him.

I've heard pastors and leaders say, "We can't look at the standard of scripture and reduce it down to try and make it meet our life experience. Rather, we are to look at scripture as a standard that we rise up to achieve." In other words, we don't look at the promises that Jesus made and "dumb them down" because we haven't actually experienced them. Instead, we are to look at the words of Jesus and the promises of God and contend for them until they become normal in our lives.

When we look at the miraculous life that Jesus lived, the standard is set really high. Just because we may not see someone always saved, healed, or set free when we pray for them, that doesn't mean it's not available for us today. We can't always understand why things happen the way they do… or don't.

## Growing in my Discovery of Healing

Early on, I had a few experiences seeing God heal someone, but I still considered them to be a rare anomaly. I was still discovering the reality of the gospel as being directly linked to people getting saved, healed, and delivered.

Just outside the gate of Universal Studios in Southern California, I was attending a conference. At each break, I would connect with other attendees and then we'd go grab a meal at some nearby restaurant. During one of the breaks, I decided to finish my meal as quickly as possible because my favorite worship band was about to lead worship in the afternoon session.

I threw the rest of my lunch away and hurried back to the venue alone. On my way, I had to pass the front gate of the theme park, and as I was walking, I suddenly felt an intense pain in both of my knees, and felt the need to stop. I looked over to my left and saw a large family sitting together just outside the park gate. Immediately a thought came into my mind, "Someone in that family has knee pain. Go pray for them" I shrugged off the thought and continued walking. The more I walked, the more intense the pain got. I looked back over my shoulder toward that family and again the thought came, "Go pray for someone in that family who has knee pain…" I realized then that it wasn't my own inner voice, but the Holy Spirit trying to get my attention.

Still, I hesitated, because I kept thinking my favorite worship band was about to play. I also felt really awkward about walking up to a group of total strangers to ask them if I could pray for them. Even as I tried to continue walking toward the venue, I realized that to walk away would be total disobedience to what I sensed God was asking me to do. Many times the greatest miracles and breakthroughs are just on the other side of our greatest fears.

I made my way back to where this family was. As I got closer, I could tell it was probably an extended family gathering together to go into the theme park. I was nervous as I approached them and had no idea what to say other than, "Hello, do any of you all have knee pain?" I stepped back and waited and they all started speaking in Spanish. I chuckled to myself and started to wonder if God had led me over to a family that I couldn't even communicate with! After a few moments, they all got excited and one of them came toward me holding something. I was a little confused, but then realized that something had been lost in translation. The person was coming toward me to hand me a pen and said in broken English, "You wants a pen?"

I thanked them but then tried to ask them one more time. I bent over and put my hands on both of my knees. Now I could see confusion on all of *their* faces. I spoke very slowly and patted my knees, "Does… anyone… have…. knee… pain?"

Suddenly they all go in a unified chorus, nodding to each other, "Ohhhhh! Knee pain!"

They laughed and I couldn't help but laugh with them. Talking in Spanish, someone explained that their grandmother sitting nearby had pain in both knees. It was such a confirmation when they explained that someone, in fact, did have knee pain—my sense from the Lord wasn't just a random idea that had popped into my head. I walked over to her and started up a conversation, quickly realizing that she spoke little or no English. The rest of her family just watched, I'm sure half amused and half confused. I tried asking her if she had pain in her knees but she had no idea what I was saying. I started to get a little worried that the language barrier was going to be too much and that I wouldn't be able to pray with her. Right then a young guy, who was also attending the conference, walked up to me and this elderly woman and asked, "Hey bro, what's going on?"

I told him the situation and the challenge I was having. He

smiled and started talking to her in fluent Spanish. He looked at me, "Yes, she does have knee pain. It's really bad." I had him ask her if we could pray. He did and she agreed. As I was praying for her, the young man talked to the woman, and when I finished, I looked at him, a bit confused as to why they were talking while I was praying for her.

He told me, "She said as soon as you started praying, her knees became very hot, like fire."

I asked him, "Really? Is that a good thing?"

He looked at her and asked her the same question. She nodded and he looked back at me, "Yes, she said it's a good thing."

Not fully understanding, I asked him to have her stand up and see how her knees were feeling. As soon as she stood up, she started doing squats and shouting in Spanish! Her family had been watching and so were people who were sitting around in the same area. I didn't have any idea what she was saying but I could tell that something had happened.

The young man leaned over toward me and translated, "Praise You God, praise You God, all my pain is gone!" She kept shouting as tears were streaming down her cheeks. She gave me a big grandmotherly hug and explained through our translator that she was worried about being at the park all day with her family because she didn't know if she could take walking around so much. She told me that after we started praying that her knees became very hot and that all of the pain immediately left! I started to thank Jesus out loud with this woman, in a different language but in very much the same spirit. That day, I realized the importance of obeying the voice of the Holy Spirit and the joy we can access when we partner with God to bring healing to others.

## God Responds to our Faith

*"And without faith it is impossible to please God..." Hebrews 11:6*

Over the past few years as I've been on this journey I have seen that God responds to and delights in our faith. Each time I pray for someone who is sick or facing an impossible situation, it requires some level of faith on my part. When I step outside of my comfort zone to pray for someone's healing, I'm demonstrating that I believe God can heal them. It's not my job to ensure someone gets healed but I do believe that God wants me to live a life of faith—that wherever I go, I'm believing Him for the supernatural.

Doing so attracts the Holy Spirit and His presence into each circumstance. I see it over and over in public places when I pray for someone to be healed. As soon as I step out in faith, I can sense the presence of God. God is everywhere all the time, but when He tangibly manifests or reveals His presence, everything begins to change. It's not that I have to "feel" something but that I am aware of His manifest presence and supernatural things begin to take place.

I'll never forget arriving for a television interview along with a number of professionals who were gathered for the taping. I enjoyed meeting people and at the end of the session, I felt the need to pray for a woman for a specific physical need. When I began to talk to her about it, I could sense her discomfort and the fact that I was crossing the unseen line in talking about prayer. She reluctantly agreed and as soon as I started to pray, I could sense the atmosphere in the room change. The people who were in the area started watching and the whole room became aware of what was going on.

I asked her how she felt and with total surprise, she told me she no longer felt what had been bothering her. What followed the experience is what makes the moment so memorable. As soon as she began to share her testimony of what God had just done, the presence of God started to fill the entire room. It was as if the reality of heaven started to permeate the area where the filming was taking place. As I sensed God's presence fill the place, I also noticed a tangible shift in the demeanor of those around me and other people started asking for prayer.

A line formed and for the next thirty minutes or so we had a time of ministry in a crowded narrow hallway. One person after another encountered the love of God and the power of God. He moves powerfully in public places and doesn't follow what we think is the social norm!

When you step out in childlike faith, the Holy Spirit responds in a special way. He reveals himself most powerfully when you share the love and power of God with those around you. They're not meant to be something we enjoy just in services. God longs for His presence and power to be released in everyday situations and places. If you read the gospels you can see that most of the miracles and healings that Jesus performed happened outside of a religious setting. When He sent His disciples out, He instructed them to heal the sick and to go to the people's homes. He could have sent them to the synagogues or to religious settings, but instead He wanted to demonstrate the Father's heart to seek and save those who are lost.

## Why Doesn't Everyone Get Healed?

I want to tackle one of the greatest questions that often comes up when I talk with others about healing and miracles. The most common question I hear is, "Why doesn't everyone get healed?" or "Why do some people get healed and others do not?" Not only have I heard this question countless times, but I too have often wrestled with this question throughout the journey of discovering God's healing power. People have written entire books about this one question and I'm not going to try and answer it entirely, but rather just share some thoughts based on my own study and experience.

Jesus healed many people in Israel in His time but also passed by many others and never healed them. Why? I think the clearest explanation is that Jesus was simply led by the Holy Spirit in everything He did and stayed laser-focused on "going about His Father's business." His primary goal was not to perform miracles, but rather was to become the sacrificial Lamb of God who would take away the sins of the world. Jesus was fully God and fully man. He was limited in every normal way that we are by time and space. He could only do so much as a man in those three years of ministry. He also had to take care of His body by sleeping, eating, and resting just like any of us. His goal each day was to simply do the will of the Father.

Jesus waited until after He was baptized by John before He performed any miracles. The first recorded miracle was when He turned water into wine at a wedding celebration in the Galilean town of Cana. From that moment on, He was launched into a collision course with the cross. His first miracle was what initiated the point of no return and when He began to be revealed to those around Him as the promised Messiah they had long been waiting for.

Many times, after performing a miracle, instead of encouraging people to go out and tell others, He commands them to say nothing. Why? I believe it was because He knew that authentic miracles and healings have major social implications. As soon as word got out that Jesus was able to perform great miracles, the crowds who followed him became overwhelming as did the number of people who wanted to be healed.

Miracles attract attention, persecution, and great need. It was only after he started doing great miracles and drawing crowds that the religious leaders started making plans to come against Him. It was also when He was performing these miracles that crowds started following Him everywhere He went. From the moment He did his first miracle in Cana, to the time he raised Lazarus from the dead in Bethany, there was a non-stop demand.

I believe that when we look at this demand on Jesus' life, we can begin to better understand one of the reasons we may not be seeing as many healings. The gift of healing and the anointing for miracles comes at a great price and demand on our lives. We see this all through the book of Acts that even the early disciples endured great persecution because of miracles they performed through the name of Jesus. We need to be prepared for great pressure if we want to see great miracles!

1 Corinthians 12:4 makes it clear that there are "different kinds of gifts, but the same Spirit. That means that the Holy Spirit is the one who decides who gets what gifts and to what measure. I believe that sometimes we do not see great miracles through our lives because our character cannot handle the weight of what will come through these miracles.

It's hard to imagine the types of pressure that would come upon us if every person we prayed for was instantly healed. It's also hard for us to realistically assess ourselves and how we might handle those pressures. For most of us, including myself, we assume that we would handle it well. God sees our hearts and the maturity that we have and how much of the anointing and the gifts we can handle. There are many examples from even recent church history of how authentic healing ministry creates an extreme amount of persecution and pressure for the person being used by God.

John G. Lake, a preacher in the early 1900's who served South Africa as a missionary[10], shares about how God started using him in a powerful way in his ministry and how it overwhelmed him and his entire family in ways that he never could have imagined. As the word spread, people began showing up day and night, almost unceasingly, to his home to receive prayer and healing. In fact, severe consequences occurred as a direct result of the added pressures in that time of his life. Do we really know how we would handle such pressures? I think one of the reasons we don't see everyone we pray for get healed is because we aren't able to handle the anointing.

I have come to this resolution about why some people don't get healed: It's my job to pray for those He leads me to and it's God's job to heal. That's it. My main focus is to seek His face and to allow Him to grow my character and maturity so that He can use me in greater and greater capacities. His kindness and mercy are not going to give me more than I can handle with Him. He knows how much favor, attention, and demand I can currently handle. I can trust that more and more He will choose to do great things through me as He desires.

## Another Common Barrier to Healing

A common barrier to people receiving healing can be their own bitterness and un-forgiveness. I've seen many times where people

---

10 Lake, John G., and Roberts Liardon. John G. Lake: the Complete Collection of His Life Teachings. Whitaker House, 2004.

were experiencing affliction and pain in their bodies that was directly connected to bitterness, unresolved hurts, or resentment. It is scientifically proven that our mental health can affect our physical health. Stress and anxiety can also create a whole list of complications and physical issues if not dealt with properly. In a similar way, spiritual sickness can affect people's bodies and souls. Many people would agree that bitterness and un-forgiveness can affect mental health, but fail to realize that it can also affect physical health.

Jesus came to bring health and wholeness to every single area in our lives—our minds, wills, emotions *and* our physical bodies. When a person is unwilling to release bitterness and forgive someone, which is a spiritual malady, sometimes as a result, they will not receive physical healing.

I remember ministering one night to a group of men in a rehabilitation program. After sharing my story, several came up for prayer for excruciating back pain. As I stepped toward one of the men, I sensed the Holy Spirit say, "He needs to forgive his brother." It was unusual and very clear. I looked at him and asked, "Do you need to forgive your brother?" He immediately started to cry and said that he did. After praying and forgiving his brother, I looked at him and asked, "How does your back feel?" To the surprise of both of us, his back felt completely better. The issue he was facing was physical in nature but was rooted in a deeper spiritual issue. While this is not always the case, it often can be a barrier to why some people do not receive their healing.

Remember, there is no formula for healing. It's something that must always be Spirit-led. As we grow in our relationship with God through the Holy Spirit, we will become more and more effective in bringing healing to others.

## Conclusion on Healing

We are *all* called to be on a journey of representing the Kingdom of God and to pray that it will be "on earth as it is in heaven." When we release healing and miracles, a taste of heaven is released on the earth. God's kingdom is coming now in part through these miracles and will one day fully come. On that day, all sickness and brokenness will be healed eternally! We must continue to press on for God's Kingdom now while we also wait with eager expectation of His Kingdom to come in its fullness when Jesus returns.

Ultimately, I have realized that God is able to do far more than I could have ever imagined. I have also discovered that at times there is great disappointment and let down when, for whatever reason, someone is not healed. Through both the highs and the lows I have resolved to believe God at His word and to continue to pray for people, expecting great miracles, signs, and wonders. It's important to remember that the Word of God teaches that not only did Jesus bring healing to others but he also commissioned his followers with authority to do the same. We must stand on the promises of the Word of God and boldly respond to the incredible promises we find there.

I'm still on this journey of discovering His power to heal and perform mighty miracles. My greatest prayer is that I resist becoming jaded in the process and hold fast to childlike faith no matter where it leads me. I want to also encourage you to be filled with faith and the love of Christ as you go share the gospel and minister healing to others. Don't be discouraged even when you don't see the breakthrough. Keep praying and believing God for the impossible!

## Final tips on praying with people for healing:

Here are some final tips that I want to share with you. I also want to challenge you to step out and pray for someone who is in need of physical healing! Let your own journey in discovering the joy of demonstrating God's healing power begin today.

1. Look to pray for people as often as possible, especially if you notice someone has a visible issue with his/her body. Be sure to ask if you have permission to pray for healing. The best way to grow in the gift of healing *is to exercise it.*

2. Ask questions before praying. I often use a scale of 1-10 to find out how bad the pain is, then ask how it feels afterward. This helps to assess what God is doing while ministering.

3. Be sensitive to God revealing the issues people around you may be experiencing. The details that you become aware of without being told are called *words of knowledge* (see 1 Corinthians 12:8). This gift often works together with the gift of healing. In the story about the woman with the knee problems, for example, God gave me a word of knowledge by allowing me to experience a brief pain in my knees. When God gives us words of knowledge for others, many times we will then see His miraculous power on display. He is all about demonstrating His love, so learn to stay alert to what the Holy Spirit may be revealing to you.

4. No matter the immediate result of prayer, I always encourage and exhort people I'm ministering to, demonstrating His love for them. Those who are not physically healed often become open to the gospel after receiving prayer and even make a decision to follow Jesus Christ!

5. Expect an instant miracle! Healing doesn't come because of our long prayers or perfect words. Healing comes because of the power that is in the name of Jesus Christ and the reality that He purchased our healing on the cross (Isaiah 53:5).

## Activity

1- Think of someone you know who needs healing in their body right now. Send them a text or give them a phone call. Ask them if they would be willing to let you pray for them. Use the tips on praying for healing as you lead them in a simple prayer. Ask them how they feel afterwards and then write about your experience below:

2- Find someone before today is over to pray for healing in person. Use the tips on praying for people for healing as needed. Write below what happened:

# 9 - DISCOVERING FREEDOM

*"Now the Lord is the Spirit, and where the Spirit of the Lord is, there is freedom" (2 Cor 3:17).*

When I think about all that Jesus did for me on the cross and the price that he paid for my freedom, I can't help but have a heart full of thanksgiving. It's so important that we all remember the price Jesus paid and what He has done for all of us. There is no greater love that could have been expressed than for Jesus to lay down His life for us. There is no greater expression of friendship. It's unfathomable the amount of love that Jesus has for each one of us. He paid the ultimate price for my freedom and for yours. He suffered and was beaten so that I could be made whole. He came so that I can have life and have life abundantly. There is no amount of words that could ever fully express the level of gratitude that Jesus truly deserves for all that He has done.

God has brought me into a measure of freedom and joy that I never would have imagined when I first surrendered my life to follow Jesus. I had no idea at the time I surrendered to Christ what to expect and what was really possible. Honestly, I couldn't imagine my life without the things that held me bound. What's incredible is that along this journey, God has graciously delivered me from so many things that were robbing me of my potential and keeping me from my destiny.

The purpose of our freedom and deliverance in Christ is so that we can walk in a way that honors God. When we obey Him and walk in His ways, we experience the greatest measure of freedom. God's desire for our obedience is not to merely put us into religious restraints but it's actually so that we can fully abide in His love and experience true freedom. It's in obedience to God and His ways that we find true life and liberty. He knows what is best for each of us and desires that we walk in the abundance of life and wholeness. He wants to remove everything from our lives that gets in the way of His love and His plans for us.

One of the ways I experienced personal freedom was related to my own intense struggle with anxiety and fear. My life was riddled with anxiety. I could not imagine a life free from it. It became so familiar that I adjusted to it on a daily basis. As a matter of fact, before coming to Christ, I was diagnosed with severe panic disorder and would have crippling panic attacks. There were times I was paralyzed with an indescribable fear.

When I arrived at a Teen Challenge program to deal with my drug addiction in 2009, intense waves of my past mistakes started coming back to haunt me. There were weekly letters from various government agencies because of the decisions I had made, the loss of all of my belongings, and my most important relationships. It was as if my whole world had caved in around me, except that now I had no drugs to help me cope with the pain and anxiety. To describe how unbearable it was would be almost impossible. I was at my wits' end and almost daily struggled with a war within my head to flee back to the familiar dregs of drug addiction.

I tried to fight my anxiety, fear, and depression as much as possible, but the more I fought, the worse it became. I was trapped in my own head and had no idea how to get out. Finally, I decided I had enough and was going to leave the program. The night before I intended to leave I had a powerful encounter with the Lord. An intern declared that God had a better plan for my life than I could imagine. As he spoke, the presence of God surrounded me and a wave of unfamiliar emotions surged through my body in a way that caused me to tremble, fall to my knees, and start weeping uncontrollably.

I felt love. I felt peace. I felt joy. I felt God's heart rushing towards me in a way that took down all of my anger and skepticism. It was a moment I will never forget because it was absolute surrender.

## Absolute Surrender

In warfare between nations, there are two ways that wars come to an end. Each side of a conflict can choose a conditional surrender and sign a treaty, or the winning side can demand an absolute surrender. For example, at the end of the American civil war, the Union Army demanded an absolute surrender from the Confederate Army. They demanded that there would be no reservations and no holding back. The Confederates were forced to surrender everything.

What I experienced was a similar moment of absolute surrender. I had attempted a "conditional" surrender with Him before where I tried to bargain with God and offer Him certain areas of my life. Each of these conditional surrenders ultimately ended up in me taking back full control of all areas and running back to the destructive patterns that had troubled my whole life. I would go back and forth in this war between wanting to do what was right and yet always falling back towards what was wrong.

Incredibly, from the moment of total surrender to the Lord, I have not had to deal with the anxiety and fear that once controlled me. When I finally gave permission for Jesus to become my "Prince of Peace," I was liberated! It was when I held onto control in certain areas, He could not be the "Prince," or leader, in those areas. To the degree that I held onto control, I was unable to experience His peace.

In order to experience the blessings of the King, we must be submitted to His leadership as a King.

Jesus taught his disciples that in order for them to find life, they were going to have to lose it. The key to discovering the joy of freedom in our own lives begins with laying down every area of our lives and dying to ourselves. It's in the letting go of control that we find true freedom and peace through Christ.

One moment with Jesus can change everything.

It's hard to read the gospel accounts and not run into a story of Jesus bringing men and women into freedom and deliverance. It's kind of shocking how many times it is mentioned in the gospels and yet how little the western church teaches on the subject of deliverance and the supernatural realm. To remove the subject of deliverance and freedom from the gospels would require you to almost take the four books out entirely. Jesus was very focused on bringing people out of the darkness and into His marvelous light. In fact, according to Luke 4, when Jesus started His ministry, He declared in the synagogue that He had come to fulfill Isaiah 61:1-2, which declares that the Messiah, or Anointed One, would come to bring deliverance, freedom, and healing.

## Jesus Came to Bring Freedom

One of my favorite places in the world to go is the Sea of Galilee in the northern part of Israel. I often think about how much I hope to revisit, even though I've been there numerous times. There is something about standing in the very places where Jesus did most of His ministry and where His disciples were recruited. Whenever I go, my favorite thing to do is to get off the beaten path and make my way up the various hillsides that surround the area. I love going up to the top of the hills because they were the places that Jesus often went up to when He sought to spend time alone with the Father. I love to go up alone, think about these passages in the Word and contemplate what it must have been like when Jesus was there praying.

During the time of Jesus, there were basically two sides of the sea of Galilee. One side was mostly influenced by the Jews and the other was by the non-jewish gentiles. There were ten cities, known as the Decapolis, that were along the eastern side of the sea. These were pagan cities and were considered to be the antithesis of everything Jewish. What's interesting is that it's recorded several times that Jesus actually took His disciples across the sea to the side where some of these ten cities were located.

In the story of Mark 5:1-20, Jesus leads His disciples over into this area and encounters a man who was demon-possessed and living in the caves that are all over the Galilean hillside. Instead of avoiding the man, as everyone else would have likely done, Jesus goes straight for him. The disciples were probably wondering why Jesus was even going close to a man who was acting like a complete lunatic, foaming at the mouth, naked, and covered in self-inflicted wounds.

As soon as Jesus came near, the demons inside the man responded and started talking to Jesus. Can you imagine the power that Jesus naturally emanated everywhere He went? His power and anointing had the demons tormented and terrified. The Bible says that they recognized Jesus as the Christ or Anointed One. It was the anointing of Jesus that repulsed the demons and had them begging Him to drive them out of the man and into a herd of pigs.

In front of a curious crowd, Jesus casted the demons out and they went into nearby pigs which ran off a cliff and into the sea. What the nearby townspeople witnessed was so terrifying that they begged Jesus to leave their region. They had never seen anything like it, nor had they imagined it was even possible. Most of the locals had spent much of their life avoiding this demon-possessed man who lived in the caves outside of their cities. There he was, in his right mind and down the hill were the floating dead pig carcasses in the sea.

With one encounter, the man's entire life was forever changed and he makes the obvious request to start following Jesus. What else could he imagine doing? Surprisingly, Jesus doesn't accept the offer and instead commissions the man to go out into the surrounding ten cities and tell everyone what had happened to him. The redeemed man became one of the first evangelists sent out to go and share the good news!

When Jesus brought deliverance to this man, He not only had the man's personal freedom in mind, He also knew the testimony would bring great glory to the Father. When God brings people into freedom, it produces powerful ripple effects that impacts more lives for the kingdom.

*"You know of Jesus of Nazareth, how God anointed Him with the Holy Spirit and with power, and [how] He went about doing good and healing all who were oppressed by the devil, for God was with Him"*
*(Act 10:38 NASB)*

## Sent to Bring Others into Freedom

*So Jesus said to them again, "Peace [be] with you; as the Father has sent Me, I also send you" (John 20:21 NASB).*

As Jesus came to bring people into freedom from the bondage of sin and darkness, so too did He send His disciples. Matthew 10:1 says, "Jesus summoned His twelve disciples and gave them authority over unclean spirits, to cast them out, and to heal every kind of disease and every kind of sickness." Jesus did not come to be the sole man to bring the Kingdom of God and to destroy the works of the enemy. Jesus came to set an example, release authority, and anoint His disciples to go and do the same.

Jesus did not cast out any demons or perform miracles before His baptism when the Holy Spirit came upon Him. It was from that time that He used His authority and walked in His anointing. He did all of His miracles because of this anointing and not because He was God. He could have done all of these things before His baptism but He chose to limit himself as a man to become a model for us.

One of our greatest ways to discover the joy of representing Jesus is to not only experience His freedom for ourselves but to bring others into freedom. We were created by God to bear His image and to bring His light into the darkness. When we shine His light and see others come out of brokenness and bondage, there is no greater joy. We were created by God to partner with Him in His plans to bring others out of the dominion of darkness and into the Kingdom of His marvelous light!

## My Journey into Freedom

For most of my life, I lived with a basic understanding that some of the things in the Bible may have happened in the past but almost nothing I read about in scripture was happening today. One of the things included in that perception was that demons, deliverance, and the spiritual realm were things of the past.

In hindsight, I'm kind of surprised that I had this perspective for so long. Growing up, my family faced some pretty intense challenges. I can remember times when I was a child where I witnessed various family members who went through spiritual warfare and attacks. Over time, I pushed it all under the "mental-health" rug and dismissed any of the supernatural or demonic elements that I had witnessed.

Years later, after I had experienced my own journey of deliverance and was a committed Christ-follower, my perspective started to change. In an intense season of studying the Word of God and praying, I started to ask the Lord about things I had read in the Bible about healing and deliverance.

I began to have vivid dreams about meeting people who were demonically possessed and I was casting demons out of them. For me, the dreams were bizarre and bordered on disturbing. It was so far out of my normal frame of reference that I had a hard time processing it. I still was thinking that such things were just something that happened in horror movies. The dreams persisted and my heart started to change. I finally asked the Lord, "Are You trying to tell me something?"

After some time in prayer, I realized that the Lord was wanting to use me in this way but needed to prepare me beforehand. I believe that because I had no examples around me or people teaching me about this, He was giving me dreams to prepare me by the Holy Spirit. I had no idea He was going to take me on a journey for the next few years of discovering the joy that we can have when we bring others into freedom.

## When it all Started

I remember piling into multiple 15 passenger vans with a whole crew from the small Bible school I was working for. All the students, staff, and interns were headed out on a two-week adventure across the country. We began our journey, stopping at various places around the country to minister. During these trips, my eyes were opened in some incredible ways. Looking back, these trips were my first true introduction to seeing the Holy Spirit move in powerful and authentic ways. I had visited many churches early on and was skeptical, especially when it came to charismatic Christianity.

We ended up making our way all the way to a program in Oklahoma for teens coming out of addiction and other life-controlling issues. Our basic plan was to host a "day camp" with games and exciting challenges for the students and a nightly revival service.

At the nightly services, we witnessed God moving in powerful ways. We would all pile into the gymnasium with all of their staff and students and spend hours each night in worship, hearing the Word of God and praying for students. His presence and power were tangible. During this particular trip, I played piano for our worship band and spent most of my time during the services behind a piano, witnessing so many of the teens' lives being dramatically impacted by the Holy Spirit.

On the last evening, almost all of the teens at the service were highly engaged. It was some of the most genuine and passionate worship that I had ever witnessed. There was one young man, however, who was totally resistant and just stared at us angrily while we shared testimonies. He had been acting the same way our entire visit and obviously wanted nothing to do with us or what we were sharing.

Toward the end of the night, we were closing with a special time for students to receive prayer by our team. I was at the piano and was watching God move powerfully in our midst. I noticed that the same young man was still staring at our team with an intense expression on his face. One of our team members went over to him and started talking to him. To my surprise, after a few moments, the young man walked up to the front to receive prayer.

The young man knelt down and suddenly a huge group of boys from the program all rushed to the altar to pray for him. Everyone who was watching started weeping, including myself. As they started praying, the boy began violently screaming and shaking, and ripped the draping on the stage that was in front of him. Everyone in the room started to pray loudly as he screamed and clawed at whatever was around him. I was too focused on playing the piano and praying to be shocked. I will never forget what I witnessed next.

The boy went completely still and everyone around him sort of backed away, wondering what is going on. Suddenly, he stood up and the other boys help him to his feet. His facial expression and countenance were totally changed. He looked and acted so peaceful, the opposite of what we had seen the whole week. He smiled and began to weep before the Lord.

One of our team members shared the gospel and prayed with him to receive the Baptism of the Holy Spirit. The joy that overwhelmed our entire team was indescribable. It was a true miracle that changed my life. Even years later, I've recounted the power of that moment with those who were there as we witnessed God's supernatural power to set people free and deliver them from demonic torment. For days and weeks after that experience, there was a renewed hunger for God amongst our whole team. We had discovered the joy we can have when we bring others into freedom!

## Faith, Fasting, and Prayer

Over the years, I have discovered three keys that have been helpful in opening the door for others to find freedom and breakthrough in Christ. It's not comprehensive but rather just a few of the things that have been the most helpful.

One of the clearest lessons we can learn about bringing freedom to others is found in Matthew 17:19-21. The disciples came to Jesus after attempting to drive a demon out of someone but were unsuccessful. Jesus responds and gives them three keys to being able to bring others into freedom: *faith*, *fasting* and *prayer.*

*"The disciples came to Jesus privately and said, 'Why could we not drive it out?' And He said to them,' Because of the littleness of your* ***faith;*** *for truly I say to you, if you have faith the size of a mustard seed, you will say to this mountain," Move from here to there," and it will move; and nothing will be impossible to you. [But this kind does not go out except by* ***prayer*** *and* ***fasting.****]*

He tells them very directly that they were not able to bring freedom because they lacked faith. Instead of focusing on the power of Jesus and the authority that He had given them, they were likely focusing on the size of the issue. There have been countless times I've been called into a situation to pray and minister to someone and felt totally overwhelmed by the issue they were facing. This can be one of the quickest ways to extinguish the fires of our **faith**. We must guard our hearts against unbelief and focus on the reality that our God is bigger than any issue someone might be facing.

Fasting has been a part of my life in a major way for the past several years. For the first few years of my life in Christ, I knew very little about fasting and rarely was taught about it. My own personal journey into living a lifestyle of prayer and fasting was birthed early on in my journey with Christ when He began to invite me to fast for a few days at a time. After a while I began reading books on prayer and fasting that filled me with courage and faith and I started really discovering the power of fasting.

Over the years, fasting has been probably the most powerful tool in my spiritual toolbox that has impacted my own journey. It's impacted me more than any other spiritual discipline and I believe it needs to be taught and encouraged more.

Fasting allows us to say "no" to the flesh and "yes" to the things of the Spirit of God. It's a practical way to teach your body that the Holy Spirit is in charge. It also directly affects the amount of spiritual authority you can walk in. When Jesus talks to His disciples about not being able to drive out the demon, He tells them the only way to gain the spiritual authority and power needed is through the pathway of prayer and fasting.

The more consistent I am, the easier it is to live a lifestyle of fasting and prayer. If you're reading this book and have never fasted, then I would encourage you to set a weekly, monthly, and yearly rhythm. The commitment to a rhythm of fasting has helped me so much in my journey. I'm not perfect in fulfilling my commitments but having them helps me to practice fasting far more than I would if I did not have them.

The greatest advantage that fasting brings in our lives is that *it directly opposes unbelief.* When you set out to fast a meal, a day, a week, or even 40 days, you are declaring war on unbelief in your life.

Consistent fasting and prayer are some of the most powerful ways to increase your faith and grow in spiritual authority. Remember, it was unbelief that kept the disciples from being able to bring freedom to the boy in Matthew 17.

When we are living a life full of faith, are committed to fasting, and spend consistent time in prayer, we are conditioning ourselves to be fully prepared to handle whatever God might send our way.

## Freedom by the Mountain Spring

A few years ago, our family was traveling on the west coast in Oregon. We were staying there to join in a powerful event in Portland and to take some time to visit some of the parks around the state. We had a free day together and elected to drive to the Oregon coast to see the beautiful coastal views. Up in the mountains there was a place on the side of the road where people would stop and draw water from a mountain spring near the road. I had never seen anything like that before and thought it might be cool to check it out on our way back.

At our destination, we spent most of our day hiking along the coast on one of the trails in a state park. The views were breathtaking. Many of the hills and cliffs ran directly into the ocean which is vastly different from the beaches I grew up going to in North Carolina and Florida.

We packed back into the car at the end of the day, and as we drove home, I realized we had no more water to drink, so I decided we would stop by the mountain spring we had noticed on the way there if we saw it again.

As we drove along the mountain roads toward Portland, we saw the mountain spring just ahead and excitedly pulled over and grabbed water bottles to fill. I stepped out of the car and noticed a man with a bunch of empty gallon jugs all lined up. There was also another car and a woman walking around the area. I didn't notice her acting unusual at first, but then saw that she was pacing back and forth and speaking to herself.

I walked over toward the water supply and as I got closer to her, she stopped pacing and stared at me. I could sense that something was off, so I slowed down my pace and smiled at her in a kind way and felt the urge to tell her that Jesus loved her. As soon as I said it, she started talking in another voice. I went back to the car and asked my wife, Ellen to come outside. She walked closer to the woman and asked what her name was and in that same voice, she told her she had no name.

The woman came over to us and we talked for a minute, then asked if we could pray for her. She agreed and as soon as we started praying it was as if her feet were swept out from under her and she flew onto her back. Immediately she starts shrieking and growling. The man who was over at the fountain drawing water looked over in total shock at what was going on. I'm sure he had never seen anything like it before. I did, however, notice he had a christian fish emblem on the back of his car. I looked directly at him and said, "please pray" He nodded his head and watched as we gathered around the woman on the ground.

Ellen and I kept our distance because we had no idea how violent she might become. As we started praying the woman stopped flailing and crying out and became eerily still. Suddenly her eyes opened and they looked clear. All of the confusion and rage was gone. The contortions of her face and body stopped entirely. Ellen asked her name and she told us. Ellen smiled and we knelt down next to her. She had no idea why she was on the ground or what had just happened to her.

We shared the gospel with her and she prayed with us and put her faith in Jesus Christ right there next to the mountain spring. Ellen and I spoke to her for a while and gave her our information. We found out that she was raised by a woman who was a satanist. She told us that she was systematically abused and tortured as a part of satanic rituals growing up. We shared with her that no matter how much darkness she had experienced, that Jesus' desire was to totally set her free and bring her out of the darkness and into His light!

## Practical Thoughts on Deliverance

There are so many more stories and examples I could share.

The more I grow to discover the kindness and love of God, the more I realize how much He wants people to be free. Not only does God want to see people set free from demons and torment but also from anxiety, depression, addictions, and compulsions. Jesus came so that we can not only get into heaven but also so we can experience the Kingdom of Heaven here and now. Wherever God's Kingdom comes into the life of a person, any darkness has to go. Jesus said that one of the ways we can visibly see the Kingdom of God here and now is when, by the "finger of God," people get set free.

I'm not looking for something to happen everywhere I go but I do want to remain open if God wants to use me this way. I also refrain from labeling someone or accusing someone who may be dealing with a sin issue, mental illness, or addiction with having a "demon." The reality is that there are a number of things that cause issues. We never want to label but to demonstrate the love of God and point people to Jesus. We must be careful not to over-spiritualize things or manipulate people by labeling them as having a certain spirit.

With that being said, I also think that many times we can mislabel someone who is demonically possessed as having sin issues or a mental health problem. This can allow them to stay in bondage because we're unwilling to acknowledge or deal with the fact that they are tormented spiritually. I've been in gatherings with some influential pastors who struggled with acknowledging the spiritual realm and demonic torment. I've also heard people over-spiritualize everything to the point where it's alarming and unhealthy. It's important that we find balance in everything and stay sensitive to the Holy Spirit.

Almost every single time I have ministered to people who were dealing with demonic torment, it was in the context of praying for them to encounter God's love and presence. I've almost never known that they were about to be delivered. When people are tormented, whatever darkness is in them is absolutely repulsed by God's loving presence. There's no need to "summon" or try to find demons in people. When we simply minister the presence and love of God to people, the darkness will naturally reveal itself and then can be dealt with in a loving way.

I've also had many experiences where demons started to manifest in people in church, including those who have been attending church for years. During those times, there seems to be a tendency to "fight" or yell at the demon, which I've never seen to be effective in bringing true deliverance. Instead, I try to get the person to look at me and coach them to say, "Jesus, set me free." The reason this is important is that almost every time I've seen demons manifest in people, the person loses total control, the awareness of what's happening, and the ability to respond. This may be hard to believe for some people, but I assure you this is a very real part of deliverance ministry. Rather than fighting, yelling at, or talking to demons, I focus on lovingly talking to the person and asking them if they would be willing to cry out to Jesus for freedom.

Many times, getting someone to cry out to the Lord is the first step in getting them free from torment. After that, I lead them through dealing with any un-forgiveness, unconfessed sin, or other issues that are revealed.

People become tormented in this way because of "doors" that were opened up through disobedience to God's Word. It's important to encourage people after receiving ministry to walk in obedience and refrain from re-opening doors that allowed the torment in the first place. I've seen people get radically delivered from demonic torment and then return back to old sin patterns and open doors to even worse torment than before (Matthew 12:43-45).

## Being Baptized in the Holy Spirit

It is essential to invite people to be baptized and filled with the Holy Spirit after we have led them into freedom. In the same way we can have faith for people to be delivered of demonic torment, we can also believe that the Holy Spirit wants to baptize and fill them after they have been set free. Jesus said in Luke 11 that it's important after they have been emptied of demons that they are then filled with the Holy Spirit so that the torment does not return.

I once prayed for a young man who came up to me after a service and as I prayed, the Lord kept speaking the word, "Santeria" to my mind. I asked him if that meant anything and he admitted that he and his entire family were involved in witchcraft. I asked if he would be willing to repent of all witchcraft and as we prayed, a powerful demon manifested. The guy now looked like he was just one second away from pouncing on me in a rage. I immediately recognized a transformation in his countenance and started to pray for deliverance. After praying for several minutes he was radically set free, the demon left and his whole body relaxed.

Afterwards, he accepted Christ and I invited him to ask the Holy Spirit to come and fill him. We waited for a few minutes and nothing happened. I sat with him for at least 20 minutes and read my Bible as he quietly waited with his eyes closed. Suddenly he shouts and I jump out of my seat, terrified by the sudden break of silence. I looked over and he was trembling under the power of God and began to speak in a language I did not understand. I knew he had been filled with the Holy Spirit in the same way the disciples were in the book of Acts.

## Discovering the Joy of Freedom

My hope and prayer is that we will continue to discover the freedom that God wants for each of us and use our lives to bring others into freedom. The amazing reality is that "if the Son makes you free, you will be free indeed" (John 8:36 NASB). Jesus is alive and is still able to set people free and fill them with the Holy Spirit. There is no depth of darkness that is too much for the light of Christ. We can stand firm knowing that God's Kingdom is greater and more powerful than anything in the kingdom of darkness.

It's hard to describe the joy I have experienced as I've been able to witness people be radically delivered. There's no joy that compares to partnering with the Lord in bringing people out of darkness and into the light. We were created to bring freedom and healing to the world around us. When we step into this, we are able to taste the joy of partnering with God to extend His Kingdom and His will into the earth.

# 10 - DISCOVERING THE JOY OF THE JOURNEY

One of my favorite hobbies is hiking and going on long adventures in nature. For me, and many others, there is something about unplugging and getting into the great outdoors that recharges my soul. As I've grown a little older and the demands of life have increased, I've found that this hobby has been vitally important to my connection with the Lord. I love to talk to God along the trails, reflect on the past, and think about things to come.

One Christmas, Ellen and I decided to celebrate by getting backpacking gear for the whole family. I enjoyed the process of researching all of the best new gear and discovering the best deals I could find. We gathered all the essential items and happily wrapped them for Christmas morning. It was a Christmas to remember. In fact, we were all so excited about the new presents that we set out that afternoon for a hiking trip! That day was the beginning of our growing family's backpacking adventures.

About 45 minutes from where we live is a 23-mile trail called Pine Mountain Trail. I had often hiked different parts of it but had never attempted to do the whole thing from beginning to the end. After our family had done a few smaller trips with our new gear, we decided that we were now ready for a bigger challenge—the whole trail with our whole family in one weekend.

We got everything packed up the week prior and bought special food that is specifically designed to last for trips like ours. Packing for a backpacking adventure can be almost as much fun as the backpacking adventure itself. Seriously!

Once we all piled into the cars, we set off for the trail with our oldest son Landon, one of his friends, our son Josiah, and our dog

Selah. We parked one car at one end of the trail and then all rode together to the other end and set out on our three-day hiking adventure.

The first day was a short hike, which was nice because we hit the trail around sundown, which limited the time to get to our first designated campsite. Hiking as fast as possible, the goal became to locate our campsite while we could still see the trail markers.

## Lost in the woods

When I was growing up, I remember getting lost in the woods after dark and not being able to find a way out. I was about 5 or 6 years old, and my dad and I, along with two other boys, were hiking on a trail near a lake. We had an incredible time together in the woods enjoying the beautiful scenery. All the fun ended abruptly when we realized the sun was setting fast on an unfamiliar trail miles away from our car. After hiking until it was too dark to discern the path, my dad realized we were lost and had no idea how to get back. We walked over towards the nearby lake and could make out the illuminated boats and houses. We sat down and ate the rest of our snacks and drank the last bit of water as we tried to figure out what to do next. It was one of the first times as a child I remember being in a situation with so much uncertainty. My dad was debating between sleeping where we were until sunrise or continuing on to try to get back to the car.

Finally we decided to use our flashlights to get the attention of some of the houses on the far side of the lake. Not knowing how effective the small flashlights would be in gaining their attention, after a half hour or so, a boat started in our direction. We frantically waved our flashlights, hoping that they would notice and come help us. The boat kept coming closer and closer toward the lake where we were stranded. When they reached us, the man asked us if we needed help and we explained that we were stranded and didn't know the way back to our cars. He said that he had noticed our lights flashing and came to see what was going on. We were so thankful! We got on his boat and he took us to the marina where we called my mom to let her know what had happened.

## Our 23-mile Journey

Now on my family's trip, we did arrive at our first campsite in time to set up everything before sunset. We got our campfire going and enjoyed our first camp meal together, and after filling our bellies, we jumped into the tent more than ready for sleep and the rest of the journey ahead of us.

Since Josiah was only 18 months or so, Ellen was carrying him in a special pack that could hold a small child. We hiked along the trail the next day for about 7-8 miles. As we got further and further along, I could tell the boys were getting tired from the long day of hiking, but we happily reached our destination and settled in for the night.

One of the important things about long hiking treks and adventures is to remind yourself to enjoy the journey and not just reaching the destination. The next two days, Ellen had to remind the younger boys of this truth and we all really had to push through the discomfort to make it through the final miles of the trail to our next designated campsite.

On our last stint of hiking, Ellen and I decided to trade packs for the day. I honestly thought I was getting the better end of the bargain carrying Josiah until I realized it had to be at least 20 pounds heavier than the pack I had been carrying. Poor Ellen had been carrying the heavier load for over half the trip, all while being pregnant!

Toward the end of the trail I was getting exhausted and the lack of sleep, normal food, and other comforts were starting to wear me down. The boys were struggling too and I was concerned about whether or not they would be able to make the final miles. I finally told them that the first ones to the end would get a prize. Suddenly their whole demeanor changed and the pains of trekking so far disappeared. They literally ran to the end of the trail and I kicked myself for not thinking of it sooner and avoiding all of the complaints we heard all along the way.

There would be no prize for me, so I just kept my focus on the next few steps of the trail. Everything in my body wanted to stop and give up but I kept going in spite of the pain. As long as I kept putting one foot in front of the other, I knew I would make it to the end. Finally, the final mile marker was in sight and the boys, standing there with their packs thrown to the ground, had joy-filled looks on their faces. We reached our goal and had done the whole trail altogether! It was something we had looked forward to accomplishing, and though it was strenuous, it was well worth the effort. Definitely a memory I will never forget!

## Lessons from the Trail

There are a lot of lessons I have learned on the trails while hiking. Our life is a lot like the trails. It's leading to an ultimate destination and while there is joy that you will experience when you reach it, you can also access joy along the way. The whole point of this book, really, is to provide practical things you can do to get the most joy possible as you live your life. No matter where you are in your journey, it's never too late to access the joy of Christ. Here are a few simple applications from the trail to bring the whole *Discovering the Joy* journey to a conclusion.

### Trails are important.

When trying to reach a destination in the woods, a trail can be helpful to avoid dangerous obstacles and getting lost. The trail helps show you the way and can save a lot of time and energy. Sticking to the trails is one of the keys to having an enjoyable hiking experience. You can venture off-trail for a time but ultimately the best way to get to your destination will always be to stick to the trail that has been tried and proven.

Trails are examples of the path you choose when you walk in loving obedience to God and His word. He has a tried and tested way of life that He has prescribed for all of humanity that is laid out in His word. Trust His ways and follow along His path, and you can be assured that you will experience the most joy.

Jesus makes it clear as to why He has given such a clear path to follow when He says, "These things I have spoken to you, that my joy may be in you, and that your joy may be full" (John 15:11).

His desire is for you to follow along on the trail He has provided, not to hinder you from "fun" or "enjoyment" but because He knows the way that will ultimately provide the most joy. When you obey God and His ways then you also access the greatest measure of Joy. Jesus said, "I am the Way..."

## Trail markers are important.

It's helpful to distinguish between the trail you are following and the one you are not. In mountainous regions of California the trails are marked with eight-foot posts so that, in case of a large snowstorm, people can identify the trails. These markers help to assure hikers that they are still on the right path. I've wasted a lot of time on unfamiliar trails, ones that have been created by other hikers who strayed away from the actual trail. At first, it was difficult to determine that I had drifted off the established trail because it can look similar. It's the markers that make the difference.

God has provided markers in our lives that tell us along the way if we're going in the right direction. Those markers can be found in His clear instructions, laws, and guidelines in scripture.

This is illustrated beautifully in Matthew 22:36-40 when Jesus was asked a question by religious leaders in the crowd listening to Him teach.

"Teacher, which is the great commandment in the Law?" And He said to him, "You shall love the Lord your God with all your heart and with all your soul and with all your mind. This is the great and first commandment. And a second is like it: You shall love your neighbor as yourself. On these two commandments depend all the Law and the Prophets."

Jesus summarized the two most important things given in the mosaic law. In Romans 13:8-14, Paul boils it down to the fact that walking in love is the way that we fulfill the law. Loving God and loving others are the two clearest markers along the path of life that helps us be sure we stay on track. God wants us to walk in loving obedience and to love others because He knows that it is the pathway to finding the most joy.

One of my favorite passages in the Bible, found in Psalm 19, details the true value of God's instructions and His provision of markers for our lives:

*The law of the LORD is perfect, reviving the soul; the testimony of the LORD is sure, making wise the simple; the precepts of the LORD are right, rejoicing the heart; the commandment of the LORD is pure, enlightening the eyes; the fear of the LORD is clean, enduring forever; the rules of the LORD are true, and righteous altogether. More to be desired are they than gold, even much fine gold; sweeter also than honey and drippings of the honeycomb (Psalm 19:7-10).*

## Trails aren't always the easiest way.

After reviewing the trail later that we had taken along Pine Mountain, I discovered that there was an easier way to get to our destination if we would have just walked along the road that follows the mountain ridge from one side of the park to the other. We put in so much effort, energy, and time to take the hard way but in hindsight, I am thankful for it.

If we would have stuck to the road, we would have missed a lot of really interesting treasures hidden out in the woods, one of which was two streams running from opposite directions into each other and forming one larger stream. It's actually the place where I asked Ellen to marry me. It's fun because each time our family hikes along that portion of the trail, I stop everyone and tell all the kids the story of how God spoke to me there and that it's the same place where we got engaged.

We would have missed seeing beautiful waterfalls, the various groves of trees, and the massive pine tree toward the end of the trail. *The joy of a trail is found in the treasures discovered along the way.*

God hasn't promised us anywhere in scripture that our lives would be easy or that everything would always go our way. We can be assured, however, that when we're following Christ, we are going to experience life to the full. When we follow along His path, there are times we will find ourselves on the harder path.

Jesus makes this crystal clear when He says, "Enter by the narrow gate. For the gate is wide and the way is easy that leads to destruction, and those who enter by it are many. For the gate is narrow and the way is hard that leads to life, and those who find it are few(Mat 7:13-14 ESV).

### Trails are only effective if they are illuminated.

As I mentioned above, trying to follow along on a trail with no daylight is a real challenge. Even with flashlights, it can be easy to get off the path and have to retrace your steps until you find the correct path in the dark. The best way to traverse any path is to do it under the illumination of the sun.

Thankfully, God doesn't ask us to follow Him without properly illuminating His pathway. It's exciting that when we have the Spirit of God and the Word of God guiding us, we can be assured that our path will always be well-lit. God's desire is for us to not get lost along the way. His word is a lamp to our feet and a light to our path (Psa 119:105).

Also, through Jesus, we can become the light to the world around us. (Matt 5:14). He not only wants to illuminate our paths but to use our lives to help guide others to the path of loving obedience that He has prepared for them. We can live with the greatest measure of joy when our lives are illuminated by God's Word and shine to help the world around us. We were created for good works before the foundation of the world and God wants us to walk in them (Ephesians 1:4).

## Discovering the Joy

God wants to be a vital part of your life's journey. You can experience the most joy along the way when remaining in connection with Him and partnering with Him to spread His joy to those around you, no matter your life's circumstance.

*Discovering the Joy* is a simple invitation to unlock joy in greater measure. It's important to note, however, that you can only unlock it to the degree that you apply them to your daily life. May you find your contentment and fulfillment in your connection with Him.

May you display His love, goodness, and truth in all you do. May you discover the joy along the journey as you lovingly obey Him with all of your heart and learn to love others with the same measure of love He has shown you.

*May the God of hope fill you with all joy and peace in believing, so that by the power of the Holy Spirit you may abound in hope (Rom 15:13).*

# ABOUT THE AUTHOR

Andrew Chalmers is an evangelist who founded the missions organization, Take the City, which is located in Columbus, Georgia. His life's mission is to abide in God's love in such a way that he would inspire others to pursue God with reckless abandon and that his life would burn so brightly that it would set countless others on fire for Jesus. He is passionate about living a life on mission with his wife, Ellen, and their growing family.

Their organization has helped to train and mobilize people to share the gospel in many churches and organizations locally, across the U.S. and all over the world. At their missions base, they host daily worship and prayer at Harvest House of Prayer. They also run Harvest Coffee, a coffee shop that is both a business and an outreach. Their ministry also has various outreaches including REDEEM, which focuses on rescuing women from sex-trafficking. Take the City's vision is to see entire cities transformed as the Body of Christ is unified and mobilized to bring the gospel of Jesus Christ.

After Andrew was radically delivered from an addiction to street drugs in 2009, he received a passion to share the love of Christ with people in cities and nations all over the world. He has had the opportunity to share his testimony and minister in places ranging from small house churches and Teen Challenge programs to stadiums with over 25,000 people.

**For more content and training resources visit www.takethecity.com**